SIX SIGMA
PRICING

SIX SIGMA
PRICING

IMPROVING
PRICING
OPERATIONS
TO INCREASE
PROFITS

ManMohan S. Sodhi and **Navdeep S. Sodhi**

Vice President, Publisher: Tim Moore
Associate Editor-in-Chief and Director of Marketing: Amy Neidlinger
Executive Editor: Jim Boyd
Editorial Assistant: Pamela Boland
Development Editor: Russ Hall
Digital Marketing Manager: Julie Phifer
Marketing Coordinator: Megan Colvin
Cover Designer: Alan Clements
Managing Editor: Gina Kanouse
Project Editor: Chelsey Marti
Copy Editor: Language Logistics, LLC
Proofreader: Leslie Joseph
Senior Indexer: Cheryl Lenser
Senior Compositor: Nonie Ratcliff
Manufacturing Buyer: Dan Uhrig

© 2008 by ManMohan S. Sodhi and Navdeep S. Sodhi
Publishing as FT Press
Upper Saddle River, New Jersey 07458

FT Press offers excellent discounts on this book when ordered in quantity for bulk purchases or special sales. For more information, please contact U.S. Corporate and Government Sales, 1-800-382-3419, corpsales@pearsontechgroup.com. For sales outside the U.S., please contact International Sales at international@pearsoned.com.

Printed in the United States of America

First Printing, September 2007

ISBN-10: 0-13-228852-4
ISBN-13: 978-0-13-228852-1

Pearson Education LTD.
Pearson Education Australia PTY, Limited.
Pearson Education Singapore, Pte. Ltd.
Pearson Education North Asia, Ltd.
Pearson Education Canada, Ltd.
Pearson Educatión de Mexico, S.A. de C.V.
Pearson Education—Japan
Pearson Education Malaysia, Pte. Ltd.

Library of Congress Cataloging-in-Publication Data

Sodhi, ManMohan.
  Six sigma pricing : improving pricing operations to increase profits / ManMohan Sodhi, Navdeep Sodhi.
    p. cm.
  ISBN 0-13-228852-4 (hardback : alk. paper) 1. Pricing. 2. Six sigma (Quality control standard) I. Sodhi, Navdeep. II. Title.
  HF5416.5.S63 2007
  658.8'16—dc22
                                                                              2007022471

To our parents, Sat Paul Kaur
and Jastinder Singh

Contents

Table of Figures

Table of Tables

Acknowledgments

Our book started with an article, "Six Sigma Pricing," published in *Harvard Business Review* in May 2005. We are grateful to *HBR* for help with that article and for permitting us to use some of the material from it.

Mohan thanks Cass Business School (City University London) for providing an environment that made this book possible. Navdeep thanks numerous colleagues and friends for encouraging him to carry out his ideas globally.

A project like this is impossible without family support. Mohan would like to thank Katarzyna, and Navdeep would like to thank Mui for support and encouragement. We owe Amelia, Ishan, and Sohum, the paternal attention they missed during the writing of this book, which was really our loss.

Last but hardly the least, we would like to thank Roger Hoerl for his comments in the early stages of this book that influenced its structure and presentation.

About the Authors

Mohan is professor and head of Operations Management and Quantitative Methods at Cass Business School in London. He has a Ph.D. from the Anderson School of Management at the University of California, Los Angeles (UCLA), with previous degrees in manufacturing and in industrial engineering. Before coming to Cass, he consulted full-time for 10 years at senior levels with Sabre, Accenture, and Scient in a variety of industries including chemicals, consumer-packaged goods, and airlines in the United States and Europe. His managerial articles have appeared in the *Harvard Business Review, MIT Sloan Management Review, the Wall Street Journal, Supply Chain Management Review, Interfaces*, and other journals.

Navdeep is a pricing practitioner and thought leader with over 11 years of global pricing experience spanning different industries: airlines, medical device, and B2B manufacturing. He has an MBA from Georgetown University. He has applied Six Sigma and Lean methods to pricing in his work for industrial manufacturers and is a recipient of the Award of Excellence from the Professional Pricing Society. His articles on pricing have appeared in the *Harvard Business Review* and the *Journal of Professional Pricing*.

Preface

It is remarkable how much the pricing of a company's products and services affects the profitability of the company in either direction: High (realized) prices can mean high total profits, and low prices can mean low total profits. From an Economics 101 perspective, there exists a perfect price at which profits are maximized, and any price lower than that point hurts not only profits but potentially revenues as well. However, in a business-to-business (B2B) selling context, there are two challenges in achieving such a price. These apply to the list price and to the price realized in individual transactions, respectively.

First, for a company with thousands, or even tens of thousands of products, it is inconceivable that its list prices are the best possible for all its products. This is especially the case in a dynamic market with continually changing competitive and customer situations. Perfect information regarding attributes and prices of all competing products is rarely available to the customer or to the company.

Second, even if a company is able to set its list prices such that they maximize its profits, each transaction has its own negotiated price or discount off the list price. Sales personnel have incentives that typically depend on the amount of sales they generate, not on the realized prices or profits. Buyers' agents have incentives that typically depend on the discounts they are able to extract off the list prices. Both sides can agree on transactions with large discounts for large sales amounts. The actual transaction price is then quite a bit lower than the list price because both sides focus on the revenue. However, such a transaction might not add to the company's profits and might even contribute to losses.

Therefore, the absence of any realistic control over transaction prices means that the company cannot realize "optimal" prices even if it can determine what these are. This absence of control can hurt in other ways too. For instance, when raw material prices go up, the company increases list prices but finds that in practice the realized prices remain the same, and so profits actually go down.

Even when there are operational controls in the company by way of price checks, requests by sales personnel to get prices approved within the company may take so long that the customer gets impatient and takes her business elsewhere. Such controls impede sales, the lifeblood of the company. As a result sales personnel, in their need to make and grow sales, have to devise ways to go around these controls. Nevertheless, circumventing price checks means that sometimes the price in a transaction is too low relative to guidelines, effectively diluting profit. Alternatively, the price may be too high relative to guidelines, hurting sales in the long term because the customer may find out and curtail his purchase in the belief that the company is opportunistic.

Improving and controlling the realized prices over individual transactions and contracts is the domain of pricing operations. If a company can improve manufacturing and service operations, why can't it improve its pricing operations? Substandard operations, whether marketing-, pricing-, or sales-related, can lead a company to distress even when there are good marketing and pricing strategies in place.

The goal for improving pricing operations is to prevent the dilution of list prices in individual transactions and contracts, assuming of course that the company has (list) priced the products correctly in the market relative to the competition and demand. Moreover, pricing operations ensure that realized prices are as close as possible to guidelines vis-à-vis list prices consistently over time and across customers. For instance, operations would ensure that volume discounts are applied consistently across transactions.

This is no different than manufacturing (or services operations) seeking to ensure that the product (or service) does not deviate from the design each time the product is made (or the service is rendered). Just as companies gain a reputation for good quality for manufactured goods or services, a company that controls its transaction prices will gain its customers' trust for superior sales and pricing practices. These customers will not suspect the company of opportunistic or sloppy practices.

There are many ways to improve manufacturing and service operations—Total Quality Management, Statistical Process Control, and Lean Manufacturing to name a few—to adapt to pricing operations. Which of these should a company follow to improve pricing operations?

To select a particular approach, one must realize that on one hand, every decade or so there is a new movement promising to rid the business world of inefficiency, which eventually becomes a fad. Companies spend much effort doing enterprise-wide implementation. Executives and consultants tell stories in business conferences while the business press writes magazine articles about stories reporting success or at least promising it. Then slowly but surely, stories of excess start circulating, foretelling the demise of the fad but paving the way for another one.

On the other hand, some ideas stay around despite the coming and going of various fads because they are core concepts and are quite useful when implemented. Such ideas include the use of statistics—inferring the state of a system or process from a sample—that permeates Statistical Quality Control, Total Quality Management and, now, Six Sigma. Another idea is incremental change or continuous improvement whether in these approaches or in Lean Manufacturing based on the Toyota Production System. This is in contrast to the radical change in Business Process Reengineering that had some successes but also birthed many disasters and unnecessary upheavals.

When we set out to write this book, our goal was not to capitalize on the current popularity of Six Sigma, but to capitalize on the ideas behind Six Sigma that predate this methodology. These ideas will survive Six Sigma when some other methodology replaces it in popularity. Therefore, when reading this book, please keep in mind that we are not cheerleaders for Six Sigma or any other movement for that matter. We are fully behind fact-based analysis and for achieving major improvements to profits through the incremental changes that underlie Six Sigma.

In regard to "incremental" changes as part of continuous improvement, what has been surprising in our own experience is that such changes in price improvements have had huge positive impacts on profitability. We might be doing Six Sigma a disservice by advertising that it aims for and achieves only incremental changes. We should clarify that the small changes refer to the changes in the process in question, not to the magnitude of benefits received.

Finally, do we need to add to the plethora of Six-Sigma-related terms with another one, namely, Six Sigma Pricing? One could say that Six Sigma Pricing is simply the application of Six Sigma to the area of pricing, which it certainly is—you can carry out Six Sigma steps for improving a pricing process as in any nonpricing application as long as you can additionally navigate the minefield that is pricing.

This, however, is where there are challenges. Pricing processes have many stakeholders, each believing he or she has a lot at stake. This means you are treading constantly on eggshells despite top management support. Not all of these stakeholders will see a Six Sigma pricing project as a win-win situation even if it adds significantly to the company's bottom line. This makes such a project vulnerable to being undone at the first possible opportunity, something that does not usually happen with manufacturing or services projects.

There are other differences between applying Six Sigma to pricing operations and applying Six Sigma to manufacturing operations. For projects related to pricing operations, the most important customers are internal. Their requirements may not be well stated or not stated at all in comparison to manufacturing projects. Pricing processes, when they do exist formally, are notable mainly for the lack of any discipline or effort to follow them.

On the other hand, pricing projects may be saturated with data, especially in comparison to services projects. Additionally, relative to the effort that goes into the project, the benefits provided by pricing projects by way of increased profits is huge in comparison to those brought by manufacturing or services projects.

Therefore, there are significant differences between a "typical" manufacturing or services situation and one that involves pricing to justify our use of the term Six Sigma Pricing. Improving pricing operations using Six Sigma Pricing is the subject matter of this book.

Part I
Motivation and Context

1

WHY PRICING OPERATIONS AND SIX SIGMA PRICING

The superior man, when resting in safety, does not forget that danger may come. When secure, he does not forget the possibility of ruin. When all is orderly, he does not forget that disorder may come.

—*Confucius (551 BC–479 BC)*

1.1 Introduction

If sales is the life blood of a company, then price is the oxygen in that blood. Yet in a 2006 interview with *Harvard Business Review*,[1] the statements of Jeffrey Immelt, CEO of General Electric (GE), are quite revealing about pricing in his company. He said, "When it comes to prices we pay, we study them, we map them, we work them. But with the prices we charge, we're too sloppy."

If the CEO of one of the most admired and process-oriented companies perceives pricing-related processes in his company as "sloppy," one can imagine things are not exactly wonderful at other companies either. GE was able to bring control to many manufacturing and services processes using Six Sigma, so why not use Six Sigma for controlling and improving pricing processes as well?

According to a November 2004 survey of 16,500 executives, "Pricing is their preeminent worry—ahead of talent shortages and operational capabilities."[2] CEOs do not feel they are in a situation to control prices at least in regard to increasing them or even sustaining them during shifts in market dynamics. As one CEO responded to an analyst's questions regarding pricing, "The business environment limits our ability to control prices."

It's true that companies can always "control" the marketplace by lowering prices, but the results can be disastrous for the bottom line. Conversely, the most efficient way to improve a company's profits is to increase the realized price of its products and services. Prices are not only influenced by external market conditions, but they are affected by less-than-perfect pricing decisions and operations within the company.

Consider the example of Lexmark International in 2005, which was enjoying growing sales in the profitable ink-jet printer segment under such brands as Dell Computers.[3] Then as sales went down when Dell lost market share for printers, Lexmark cut prices up to 30% in some brands to gain sales growth—but ended up simply losing margin and had to cut 275 jobs. At the same time, rivals Hewlett-Packard, Canon, and Seiko posted better results. Indeed, pricing decision-making and expertise are integral to a company's ability to succeed and survive.

Controlling prices refers not just to the marketplace, but also to the internal processes that have as their final output the ultimate realized price from the customer in any specific transaction. This book focuses on improving these internal pricing processes in the context of business-to-business selling. These processes encompass setting transaction-specific discounts as well as creating pricing-related clauses within contracts that affect realized prices in future transactions. Companies need to look internally at these processes to improve realized prices and stem revenue leaks.

No matter how competitive and difficult the marketplace is, much can be done within the company to improve the overall level of prices by controlling price variation and thus improve revenues. Hence, pricing expertise comprises not only the ability to devise a pricing strategy, but also to manage internal processes to adhere to this strategy.

Companies are typically not bad at controlling manufacturing or service processes or at improving operations in general. Many companies have become skillful at managing costs and improving manufacturing efficiencies. The TQM and Six Sigma movements have seen to that. Six Sigma has been used in many global companies such as Motorola, Allied Signal, General Electric, and Citibank to name a few. There is broad interest in many different industries.

However, the discipline so often brought to the cost side of the business equation is usually lacking on the revenue side. As a result, many companies continue to leak cash from the top line sales because of "defects" in the form of excessive discounts in some transactions or in the form of opportunistic high prices in other transactions that lead to customer dissatisfaction and consequent loss in future sales. Many companies are already adept or are learning to be adept at improving controls on their manufacturing and some service processes with homegrown Six Sigma expertise. We show in this book how to leverage the expertise in decreasing manufacturing defects and variability to improve pricing processes.

There are several good books, primers, and handbooks for Six Sigma and TQM, but none address pricing operations or processes. Pricing is quite different from other application areas in its context and warrants adaptation of Six Sigma (or any other methodology) developed for manufacturing or services. Likewise, there are books on pricing, but surprisingly none focus on pricing operations, let alone discuss how to improve pricing processes with better controls or other adopted methods. This book shows how Six Sigma Pricing can help improve internal pricing operations—and thus profits.

1.2 Who Should Read This Book and How They Should Read It

This book has four parts. *Part I* is about the motivation behind our approach and the payoff in improving pricing operations. We recommend this part to all readers. *Part II* provides basics of pricing operations as well as basics of Six Sigma. It will be particularly useful for MBA students or others new to pricing. *Part III* provides details of applying "Six Sigma Pricing," as we call our adaptation to Six Sigma regarding pricing. It is especially relevant for those who will be carrying out or overseeing such projects. This part is the heart of this book, showing how you can use a fact-and-data-based approach to improve operations by designing better processes and controls. The final part, *Part IV*, is about enterprise-wide deployment of Six Sigma projects and targets senior managers who need to understand enterprisewide ramifications.

The key target audience for the book are business leaders who would like to instill internal discipline and improved capability for pricing. Senior managers will learn how they can improve realized prices by bringing pricing under control. CFOs and other senior managers working on Sarbanes-Oxley issues can validate and set controls on their companies' sales or compensation processes, if related to pricing in any way, using the principles described in this book. For these managers, Parts I, II, and IV of the book should be particularly relevant.

Part III of the book provides the details for applying Six Sigma Pricing or other fact-and-data-based methodologies that improve internal pricing processes, which should be very helpful for mid-level managers involved in carrying out or overseeing Six Sigma Pricing projects. A detailed example called "Acme," based on our experience with a few different companies, supports each chapter in this part. Managers will also find supporting evidence for building a business case for such projects in Part I as well as lists of business processes in Part II.

Pricing practitioners and strategists within companies can use this book to bring colleagues together from various functions to explain pricing operations and to define roles in order to streamline pricing within the company among different functions and between the company and its customers. They can view Six Sigma Pricing as a framework to help align multiple functions to common objectives and help functions work together. They should at least skim through Parts I and II to understand how pricing operations can support or foul up any pricing strategy. They can then read Part III to see how to improve internal pricing processes, and they may find Part IV useful in drawing up enterprise-wide plans for improving pricing operations.

Consultants with pricing backgrounds will discover a practical approach to help their clients manage pricing operations better, thereby actualizing the pricing strategies they are recommending. These consultants already have tools and frameworks to understand the marketplace and to extract better prices. They can enhance their value to clients also by considering internal processes and ways to improve realized prices consistently. For them, Parts III and IV can be quite useful, while Part II can help delineate internal and external aspects of pricing.

Six Sigma experts will find in this book yet another domain within the enterprise to apply their expertise. These experts have made tremendous and well-documented contributions to the organization, not just in manufacturing but for such varied services as internal audit, customer service, and IT services.[4] These experts will find that using Six Sigma for pricing can have a huge impact even with small projects.

They should read the chapters on pricing and pricing operations in Part II of this book carefully to familiarize themselves before they get into Part III to see how their Six Sigma expertise applies to pricing.

Finally, business school students, primarily those in MBA programs and those with marketing interests, can also benefit. Business schools are sometimes accused of emphasizing theory to the neglect of practice.[5] Our book addresses two gaps: We introduce students to pricing operations as a marketing topic and in the application of an operations management tool for process improvement, namely Six Sigma. Both Part II and III should be part of the same course. The final Part IV would be especially valuable if supported by case studies involving enterprise-wide deployment of Six Sigma, TQM, or Lean Manufacturing.

1.3 Why Target Pricing Operations

Almost every marketing primer starts with the *4Ps* (product, price, promotion, and place), the marketing decision variables or marketing mix that are in a company's control. Getting this mix right is critical in order to successfully market and sell a product. Yet few companies are confident that their pricing practice can execute to their business strategy with consistency. Companies constantly invest resources in modifying pricing tools, methodologies, information systems, and training to address an ever-changing market place.

These companies do so because of the significance of price improvement to the bottom line. Consider, for illustration, an income statement with $100 in revenues, $80 in cost of goods sold, and $10 in selling costs. Then the corresponding 1% increases in earnings before interest and taxes are 8% for a 1% drop in cost, 1% for a 1% increase in volume, and 10% for a 1% increase in price. Table 1-1 shows the relative impact of improving the realized price. Therefore, it makes sense to target pricing among the three options to have the most impact on the bottom line. Of course, this is not easy, and it is the purpose of this book to show how to improve price realization by building better internal controls.

Table 1-1   An Illustration Showing Impact of Price Increase Relative to Unit Sales Increase or Cost Decrease

Income Statement Item	Actual Amount	Amount Projected with 1% Decrease in Costs	Amount Projected with 1% Increase in Volume	Amount Projected with 1% Increase in Prices
Revenues	$100	$100.0	$101.0	$101
Cost of goods sold	$80	$79.2	$80.8	$80
Selling costs	$10	$10.0	$10.1	$10
Earnings before interest and taxes (EBIT)	$10	$10.8	$10.1	$11
Percent increase in EBIT	—	8%	1%	10%

Similar analysis has been done by various consultancies on different groups of companies like 2,463 companies in Compustat (by McKinsey) and the S&P 500 (by A. T. Kearney).[6] The results are different for the two sets of analyses, but both indicate price as proportionally the most important driver for profits (see Table 1-2). On an average, a 1% increase in price without a drop in volume can lead to operating profit improvements of 11.1% for the Compustat companies and 8.2% for the S&P companies. The corresponding increases for 1% improvements in variables costs, sales volume, and fixed costs are much lower. Essentially, because price enhancements carry no corresponding increase in costs (for example, potential variable cost associated with increased volume), they flow directly to the bottom line.

Table 1-2   Average Impact of 1% Improvement of Driver on Operating Profit

Driver	Compustat Companies	S&P 500 Companies
Price management	11.1%	8.2%
Variable cost	7.8%	5.1%
Sales volume	3.3%	3.0%
Fixed costs	2.3%	2.0%

(Source: Phillips 2005: p. 14)

Despite price being so important, it is also something over which companies feel they have the least control. Clearly, given that the lack of control on pricing is mostly within the company, pricing operations is an area where companies should assert control to bring about price improvement.

1.4 Pricing Challenges and Six Sigma Pricing

There are many challenges pertaining to pricing processes within the company that cause "defects" by way of excessive discounts or excessively high prices, sometimes even to the same customer. Excessive discounts hit the top line and bottom line of the company directly. Excessive realized prices may appear attractive to the company, but customers eventually do find out if the seller has charged different divisions markedly different prices for the same product or has offered other customers higher discounts without clear explanation. These customers affect revenues by either leaving or decreasing their business, or they affect profitability and price by negotiating for extra discounts in future transactions.

Defects in pricing can be detrimental to a company's growth prospects in the long term as well. Band-aid solutions that do not fix the cause only worsen the situation. Negative experiences feed customers' perceptions that a company is difficult to work with as a partner. The occurrence of defects erodes confidence among stakeholders internal to the company as well. For example, pricing and sales personnel may offer extra discounts if they are not sure about the validity of a price point when customers complain, thus eroding margin.

Business strategy developed in the boardroom might be brilliant, but poor execution means poor results in regard to realized prices or profitability. Senior managers may feel they do not control prices because of external market factors. However, they can bring about internal discipline to control several internal factors that contribute to the gap between strategy and execution.

Six Sigma Pricing can provide this internal discipline. Even if a company applies Six Sigma Pricing to pricing operations and to transactions, shared understanding of the pricing-related roles of different groups and individuals helps in strategic pricing as well.

Let us first look at challenges that relate to pricing and pricing processes. It is these challenges that engender price-related defects.

Challenge 1: Interfunctional Divergence

Usually, processes within a single function or even across two functions tend to have good controls. Whenever we have more than two functions, it may be the case that the functions do not have the same perception of the process or its objective. This is the case with pricing processes in marketing, finance, sales, and product management because of overlapping roles and ownership, at least in the members' perceptions.

Stakeholders in various functions and levels within the company do not necessarily have the same objectives. *Salespeople* compensated on sales volume want flexibility in pricing so they can increase volume wherever there is an opportunity to do so. Marketing people are the brand builders guiding the value of a product. This can put them at odds with sales personnel who might think the list price (or proposed contract price) is too high to bring in large volume. *Pricing personnel* may use their analysis to present their view that the proposed transaction price or proposed contract price is too low relative to existing similar products. *Finance personnel* may raise questions regarding why realized or proposed prices cannot be higher than their current values.

The pricing function attempts to impose controls on prices to focus on overall pricing. However, different functions may have incentives to bypass these controls when it does not suit their objectives or their view on what would benefit the company in the future. Senior managers who could resolve these interfunctional conflicts may not be close enough to the operational level of pricing in many companies to intervene every time. Unresolved issues render price controls in these companies ineffectual and the processes ad hoc.

Pricing-related processes are also ad hoc in many companies because there is lack of a shared understanding of the role of pricing and of pricing processes. These companies have not paid much attention to pricing as a function. Therefore, results that a company obtains are not necessarily commensurate with the investments made in hiring senior-level pricing managers and in implementing pricing software technology. Use of technology in environments where interfunctional divergence is reflected in poor controls on pricing and in poor shared understanding of the pricing process is only an ill-conceived panacea.

Still there are industries with pricing operations expertise, for example car rentals and airlines, that have learned to consistently extract positive, if lean, margins even in bad times. The good news is that in other industries, attention to pricing operations is growing. Some companies now have managers and directors of pricing strategy, even Chief Pricing Officers. The number of consulting firms and pricing software companies grows by the day.

Six Sigma Pricing can focus this attention to help the different stakeholders understand pricing operations and bring different functional perspectives together. It uses data and facts to provide a framework to review and design close-looped processes.

Challenge 2: "The Customer Is Always Right"

A customer-focused company always looks for better ways to serve its customers. However, being customer-responsive is not the same as being customer-focused. Customers want quick turnaround on pricing decisions, and there is no reason why it should not be so. But, when a company has tens of thousands of transactions a year, this can create pressure to lower the price in two ways. If a company does not have solid pricing processes, its personnel may give in too easily and too quickly to requests for lower pricing for a particular single transaction, or worse, over many transactions by improving contract terms.

The "need-for-speed" in responding to the customer can translate into putting aside any due process for a transaction or putting aside any consensus-building efforts around a contract's terms. The customer's assertion of the price being "wrong" or too high can go unchallenged in this situation in the absence of any fact-based analysis.

There may have been a genuine case of a wrong price in the past. System glitches, changes in personnel at customer or vendor location, changes in competitive offering, and miscommunication are among many other known problems that exist in a business environment. Sometimes a customer learns of another customer receiving an inexplicably low price from the vendor. When a sales representative is not sure of the problem source, either scenario spurs a discussion around dropping the price in the interest of keeping the customer happy.

In the absence of a systematic framework, being responsive to the customer invariably leads to the customer extracting a lower price or less favorable terms from the seller's viewpoint. Six Sigma Pricing provides for a fact-based systematic decision process that leads to consistent prices and a focus on the customer's needs rather than always simply lowering prices to be "customer-responsive."

Challenge 3: Continual Internal and External Changes

Pricing is complex also because of its sensitivity to the continual changes in the internal and external environment. Internally, a company may have seen turnover or may have brought in new leadership, resulting in changed policies. Every changed policy can entail changes in pricing processes, and the company might not train everyone in the new process.

Externally, economic cycles or massive changes, such as the 2005 oil-price increase, change customer needs and drive the company's response. External events like mergers and acquisitions have internal impacts. For instance, existing IT systems and legacy processes with specific customer accounts or products (owing to a merger with another company for instance) make controls difficult because of integration-related challenges.

Even in stable environments, many companies make unnecessary changes in processes and organizational structure that create undesirable variations in the output of their processes, particularly in the pricing. As with manufacturing or service processes, "variation is evil" for pricing processes as well.[7] This is because the variations resulting from inconsistencies in pricing decisions lead to highly varying prices with low overall levels. Setting the price or discount for any transaction or setting terms for any contract should be a repeatable and consistent process—having variations can only lead to "defective" prices that are too high or too low. Companies need to appreciate that pricing processes should be consistent and repeatable, not just for transactions or standard contracts, but also for one-off deals for customized products.

Six Sigma Pricing can help bring control to operational processes to design and redesign transaction-level pricing processes. After all, the process to change processes is a process too and one that should be repeatable even in a dynamic environment.

Six Sigma Pricing assists in standardizing the pricing process. It helps ensure that the flow of communication from the customer to the salesperson through pricing and IT systems is smooth and timely and occurs in a closed loop system with controls that include defined exceptions for flexibility. Having standardized processes also helps with contingency planning if something were to go wrong. Standardization helps decrease inconsistencies in pricing while allowing the flexibility salespeople need to pursue sales opportunities and to close transactions profitably.

Challenge 4: Management by "Gut-Feel"

Managers may make pricing decisions based on their intuition (informed by vague memories of demand curves in Economics 101), and drop prices to increase unit sales or increase list prices to increase dollar sales. Such thinking is not wrong on a fundamental level, but the devil is in the details of execution: How sensitive is the "market" to price changes in one particular transaction? After all, an increase or decrease in list prices is one thing, the ability to realize a proportional change and desired result over thousands of transactions is quite another.

When dealing with a customer's influence on pricing, wouldn't we have more confidence in each situation if we knew the customer's purchase history, geographical location, and discount levels before addressing the customer's needs? Likewise, proposing large discounts to customers based on gut-feel about "tough times" would be on a more solid basis if such proposals were additionally based on analyzing the impact on profitability—vis-à-vis the likelihood of losing such sales.

Six Sigma Pricing helps supplement a decision-maker's gut-feel with fact-based evidence and analysis. Data-driven and fact-based evidence can take the emotion out of meetings where everyone has a different gut-feel. Doing so also results in consistent execution regardless of who is making the decision.

1.5 What Six Sigma Pricing Is

As discussed, many factors contribute to defects in pricing processes. The fundamental causes are poorly designed or even unspecified processes. But even if the processes are known and clear, controls may not be effective. Either way, the Six Sigma approach for improving processes can help.

The Six Sigma philosophy, using data and statistical tools to systematically improve processes and sustain process improvements, can be applied to the pricing process with a focus on eliminating the "defects" of excessive discounts or excessive prices. Six Sigma is a methodology traditionally used in manufacturing to improve quality. Six Sigma Pricing, or the application of Six Sigma to pricing, enables systematic elimination of process-related defects by exposing the sources of these defects.

The five stages of Six Sigma Pricing are the same as that of Six Sigma except that they are adapted for pricing processes:

- **Define** the pricing-related "defect" in operational-, transaction-, or contract-specific pricing processes and the extent of the defect.
- **Measure** the extent of the defect along with parameters of the pricing processes as well as the invoice, say by analyzing past invoices.
- **Analyze** the data collected in Measure to infer how the size or incidence of defects varies with different aspects of the pricing processes as well as brainstorm on the other causes of defects related to the existing process.

- **Improve** the process by making process change recommendations along with quantitative estimates of how much improvement in related prices or other metrics would take place following implementation of these changes.
- **Control** the proposed process. For example, recommend controls to ensure that people are following the agreed-upon modifications and that the estimated benefits are achieved.

1.6 What Six Sigma Pricing Is Not

Six Sigma Pricing is not intended to create a pricing strategy, but to improve pricing operations and adherence to an existing strategy. It applies to pricing operations and *repeated* processes, that is, to control discount levels off list prices in contracts or in individual transactions. It is not intended to define the company's position as it regards price and product attributes in the market.

A company usually centralizes its pricing strategy-setting effort—such processes tend to be tightly run, although they do not occur frequently during a year. However, setting prices for individual discounts for the tens of thousands of individual transactions in one division in a year and even creating contracts for many customers is necessarily decentralized. Such an environment can have breakdowns in control and resulting revenue leaks. It could therefore benefit from the improved controls and discipline that Six Sigma Pricing can bring. Even periodic list-price-setting across thousands of products is a repetitive process that Six Sigma could improve.

Six Sigma Pricing is not about yielding control to the pricing function or to sales personnel, although it does entail giving sales and other personnel flexibility to respond quickly to the customer. Giving personnel flexibility does not mean giving up control. In fact, using Six Sigma Pricing, companies can create tighter controls, escalating guidelines for salespeople, sales managers, and pricing personnel for discounts. Thus, Six Sigma Pricing can help companies create the right balance between flexibility and faster responsiveness on one hand and tight controls of the price on the other.

Six Sigma Pricing projects are not focus groups or jawboning sessions. Such a project involves using tried and tested robust statistical tools and other mechanisms. Furthermore, each stage has its own set of tools applicable to different situations, which we discuss.

Six Sigma Pricing is much more than designing and using improved measurement and control. It is a systematic process of building a shared understanding and the rationale for improved measurement and control. Good measurement and reporting are quite useful in controlling any process whether or not related to pricing. However, achieving this is easier said than done. The most challenging problem for CEOs is bringing about change in an organization, and Six Sigma helps with that—improved measurement and reporting are merely outputs.

Six Sigma Pricing is not about controlling only excessively low prices but also excessively high ones. Cowboy managers "taking risk" in setting very high prices or exceedingly low discounts off the list price in a particularly opportunistic transaction can be part of the problem rather than the solution when it comes to pricing. An excessively high price can be a problem especially because the customer may eventually find out about discounts offered to other customers and even to different groups in the same company. A company's gains come from the various sales and pricing personnel consistently sticking close to desired discount levels off list prices around relevant segmentation variables such as industry of the customer served, size of customer, size of transaction, and geographic location, rather than "bold" decisions by mavericks. Six Sigma Pricing helps achieve this consistency.

1.7 Summary

Pricing is critical to a company's success, and realizing a slightly better price overall across all transactions has a tremendous impact on the bottom line for any company. As such, improving prices and preventing price erosion in transactions or contracts should be the first priority for a company seeking to improve its profits.

However, many senior managers feel they have no control on prices because they cannot control external factors such as escalating raw material prices or tightening customer budgets. They need to realize that internal issues impact realized prices as well, and they can control these.

These internal issues pertain to pricing-related challenges that cause "defects" in terms of transaction prices being excessively low (or excessively high). These challenges stem from (1) pricing spanning multiple functions and therefore being subject to interfunctional conflict, (2) excessive emphasis on customer responsiveness, sidestepping internal consensus-building and analysis, (3) continual external and internal change, including ad-hoc processes, and (4) management-by-gut-feel that is different for different individuals in the absence of data-driven fact-based analyses.

The heart of the problem is the absence of well-defined processes or the absence of functioning controls even if the processes are well designed and well intentioned. Six Sigma is an approach that has done wonders for manufacturing and for services in improving processes to reduce defects.

The real purpose of Six Sigma Pricing is to help the CEO develop a shared understanding and rationale for improved control and thus manage change to improved pricing processes.

2

PROFIT LEAKS FROM INEFFICIENT PRICING OPERATIONS

For the skeptic there remains only one consolation:
If there should be such a thing as superhuman law,
it is administered with subhuman inefficiency.

—Eric Ambler

2.1 Introduction

One thing the stereotypical Economics 101 or even the typical marketing or pricing course does not describe is the inefficiency related to pricing processes. This inefficiency results in loss of profits.

In Economics 101, price is a variable that a company can vary continuously and see a related increase or decrease in unit sales along a nice clean line that reflects the price-quantity relation. This is conceptually elegant but does not represent the reality of a company engaging in hundreds of business-to-business (B2B) transactions every day for different products between sales personnel or other agents representing the seller and buyers or procurement personnel representing the customer. The price is determined across the table between individuals whose interests and incentives may not be in alignment with the profitability of their companies. Companies have checks and balances but, by definition, those who design and enforce controls and those who have to comply with these controls have different incentives.

In many large companies, sales personnel typically have incentives that depend on the amount of sales they generate, not on realized price or margins. Therefore, even when profits look grim, someone may propose doing a price promotion to increase sales. The company then ends up with not only lower profits but also lower revenues even if unit sales go up.

Sales personnel have to extend discounts to corporate buyers whose incentives are based on how much discount they are able to extract from the company. Therefore, when the cost of raw materials rises, the company tends to increase list price of products, but sales personnel find themselves having to offer bigger discounts to the buyers. As a result, the realized prices do not go up, and profits actually go down.

Controls or incentives based on margins are difficult to implement because manufacturing and distribution costs for products in a company with thousands of SKUs, even when formally allocated to each product line, are often only directionally accurate. Therefore, it is hard to create incentives based on margins.

Thus the focus is really on revenue by way of initiatives to increase it through product promotions and other special deals. These deals dilute the price from desired levels, sometimes with good reason and sometimes not. Even when there are controls in the company via price checks and price-approval requests, negotiations between Pricing and Sales within the company take so long that the customer often gets impatient and takes her business elsewhere. Therefore, even when a product has the right list price in relation to the overall market and competition, the company may not actually be able to realize this price in practice.

The dynamics of such a situation can result in price erosion from the selling company's viewpoint, resulting in lost revenues and lost profits. Let us consider some examples.

2.2 Examples of Price Leaks

In the B2B setting, buyers tend to be quite organized at negotiation, at least in comparison to sellers. Recall Jeff Immelt's comment about GE studying the prices they pay carefully but being "sloppy" at the prices they charge. The following are some specific examples of "sloppiness" in many companies:

- Customer had paid less for a product at one time and so feels entitled to that price indefinitely. A simple mistake by the pricing analyst or customer service in the past can entitle the customer's purchasing manager to repeated, unwarranted discounts.
- Pricing analysts or customer service representatives with access to cost and pricing tables in the quotation system sometimes naively help their friends in sales to get approvals for extremely low prices. Although the sale may go through as a result of the low price, the company's profits would be hurt not only for this particular sale but also future transactions with this and potentially other customers as well.

- A salesperson promises a low price to the customer, which is outside his or her decision authority, without following an approval escalation process with their superior or with Pricing. Even in companies that have a well-defined escalation process, a sales representative may get low-priced transactions through by simply stating they followed the escalation process! In such cases, the lack of effective controls renders the process ineffective.
- Sales or customer service personnel may be able to keep a quote active in the sales or quotation system long past the "valid until" date so the quoted prices can be used for months or even years without having to go to Pricing again for approval. Hence, deep discount promotions may remain alive and companies continue to leak revenues forever.
- There are IT system-related issues where a process breakdown does not allow an item to be priced correctly or a human error permeates in the system unnoticed. A customer service rep under pressure to quote tens of transactions can make an error or just make up a number that could be quite different from the correct price. Even in the airline industry, known for its IT sophistication, some large U.S. carriers have been forced on a few occasions to sell tickets worth hundreds of dollars for pennies because of errors in their web posting.

This is not an exhaustive list of examples of situations with price leaks. Thankfully, not all these leaks happen in all companies at all times. However, when such a leak does occur in a specific transaction randomly, the company may continue paying for it long after it has been detected and fixed. Such price leaks are process issues, and some may be problematic from a Sarbanes-Oxley compliance viewpoint as well because the company is exposed to risk when individuals can circumvent controls for personal gain.

Consider some examples from the airline industry, the medical supplies and equipment industry, and the manufacturing industry. Companies of these industries can have pricing "defects." These industries have widely different characteristics in regard to gross margins as well as their ability to retain as much of this margin as possible for themselves (see Table 2-1). The differences in gross and net margins depend on the different cost structures and selling processes in these industries. It is in these selling processes where controls and process compliance vary and where price leaks occur. We would like to believe that the slimmer the margins in an industry, the more meticulous they would be in managing not only their costs but also their prices.

Table 2-1   Gross Margins and Net Margins in Different Industries

Industry	Gross Margin	Net Profit Margin
Airlines	24.8%	6.3%
Medical Equipment and Supplies	62.2%	19.3%
Construction and agricultural machinery	22.3%	11.6%

(Source: Reuters.com, October 16, 2006)

Airlines

The airline industry is one that sees low margins in most years and that has a main product with a short life span—an unfilled seat. As a result, airlines are quite adept at pricing with day-of-week analysis, targeted short-term promotions, yield management, and dynamic pricing. Airlines also have had the experience of bruising price wars. Continual market review processes to identify areas of opportunities are the industry norm.

As a result, pricing or revenue management is a critical and influential function within the airline industry. The function may reside in different functional groups depending on the company—in the United States, one large airline houses Pricing within its Finance group and another has Pricing as a part of Marketing.

Despite the airlines' attention on pricing and their highly analytical approach to it, even large airlines can sometimes experience serious problems stemming from inadequate control and from customer-facing groups having incentives not aligned with growing the company's profits.

Consider one particularly egregious example: A major U.S.-based airline found that it was losing money in one Asian country despite strong brand recognition and good connections between the main cities in that country to popular U.S. locations. The company's fares to fly from that country to the United States were also lower than prices for flying from the United States to that country and back. Despite all these reasons, other airlines in the market based in that country were doing better even though they had matching or slightly higher prices.

Various reasons were put forth to explain the situation while the airline kept losing money in that market. One was that people from the country were "nationalistic" and preferred their national carriers. Another was that service quality on the national airlines was better and that the people from that country liked the food served by these airlines. With two-thirds of the passengers flying to and from that country being nationals of that country, such "nationalistic preferences" would definitely hurt.

However, as in many other situations, these so-called cultural differences did not hold water when the airline started analyzing the patterns of bookings and discovered the root cause. When analyzing the fill rate against the number of days to departure, the company found a puzzling pattern: The number of booked passengers did not follow the traditional S-shaped curve over the three months preceding a flight but instead grew rapidly in the two weeks before the flight (see Figure 2-1). The bookings for that country are also S-shaped, but the pattern is still markedly different.

Typically, the airline would expect more than 70% of the seats to be already booked 30 days before a flight departure, but for the airline's flights booked in this country, the number was 20–30%. The company would expect the number to grow slowly in the last 30 days before the flight to about 80%. However, for flights from this country, the percentage of booked seats first grew slowly to about 40% and then rapidly to the same 80% or so in the last 14 days before the flight. This was hard to explain with food preferences or other "cultural" differences.

One could argue that the rapid growth in the two weeks before the flight was a result of the deep discounts that the airline was offering, but further investigation showed that the passengers were not getting these discounts in full.

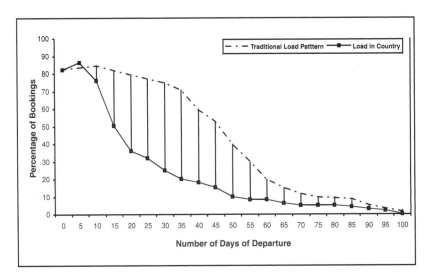

Figure 2-1 Percentage of seats booked (load) over 100 days prior to departure for a flight from the Asian country to the United States compared to the traditional booking curve for the same route

The airline eventually found that independent travel agents in that country had found a weakness in the pricing process to make more money for themselves—at the expense of the airline. The agents knew that the airline would offer deep discounts as most seats remained unfilled days before a flight left the ground. The reason was that the U.S.-based headquarters would put pressure on their local staff to "grow" the market in addition to the usual pressure to fill every seat. The travel agents figured they could delay booking passengers until just a few days from departure to get the airline to lower prices. They would then book the passengers at a higher price, still competitive to the other airlines, and pocket the difference between what the airline offered them and what they in turn offered the passengers. As a result, the plane would normally fill up by the time of the departure, but the revenue per seat mile was quite low. There are more similarities across cultures than there are differences when it comes to money!

Incidentally, the pressure to "grow" the market is a powerful motivation for deep discounting. This may sound reasonable but actually results not just in lost profits but also in poor controls that may benefit some groups or individuals at the expense of a company's profitability.

There are instances of less severe problems in this industry related to its otherwise sophisticated use of IT. For instance, a major U.S. airline experienced price leaks many years ago because of erroneous discount codes in an "open" system. A customer or travel agent would call for a discount. The customer service representative, working under intense pressure, would input a wrong reason code or simply make one up. (In our experience, customer service and managing baggage handling of incoming flights are among the most stressful jobs in the airline industry.) The system would allow the transaction to go through with the discount. As a result, the company kept losing money. More than that, tracking reports reflected incorrect trends, affecting decisions and planning. Thus, lack of process compliance stemming from erroneous codes and weak IT system controls resulted in revenue leakage through more than one path.

The company eventually identified many of the problems and put fixes in place. They started tracking results with the help of control charts with visibility to senior management. Thus, management fixed the problem at the root cause, and their diligence in following up made the improvements permanent—this is something that the Six Sigma Pricing approach addresses.

Medical Devices

The medical devices industry has high gross margins and net profit margins relative to airlines (recall Table 2-1 earlier). Given these gross margins, there is greater emphasis on increasing revenues and market share than there is on lowering costs or maintaining the price. Such an emphasis leads to poor pricing controls. Unlike the airlines that cater mainly to end customers, medical companies may have most of their business (approximately 70–75%) in contracts with hospitals, with or without intermediaries involved. The resulting transactions have discounts and rebates dependent on volume commitments in terms of absolute sales volume (units or dollars) and on year-on-year growth in the future.

At a multi-billion dollar company, weak internal processes for tracking volume and growth commitments created price leaks as the company kept giving discounts as per the contract even when the volume and growth were nowhere near the thresholds specified in the contract. This was well known in the company, but matters are papered over by customer-facing people with logic based on "let's keep the customer happy" and "don't rock the boat."

However, noncompliance with contracts created a culture where such defects were acceptable to all parties and were expected by the customer. Indeed, many customers soon figured out that contract terms were simply a bargaining tool at the beginning that they could ignore when it came to transactions conducted on a daily basis. Eventually, the company was shocked when a consulting firm informed them that they would have added $60 million annually to their bottom line had their transactions complied with the terms and conditions of their existing customer agreements!

Another malaise in this industry affecting price realization is spot pricing, similar to the airline pricing, in the form of month- and quarter-end deals. The purchasing or supply managers (or intermediaries representing hospitals) understand and exploit this behavior as part of their buying process. Many prefer to buy product in bulk at sizable discounts close to the end of a financial reporting period or simply refuse to buy unless they get the month-end deal price for every transaction regardless of when they make it. The sellers complain but find themselves desperately reliant on the month-end, quarter-end, and year-end deals that they themselves have created. These deals also create havoc with manufacturing plans by contributing to the so-called bullwhip effect, i.e., the increasing fluctuations of weekly order sizes as we go upstream in the supply chain from customers towards plants. Small changes in demand at the customer end due to price incentives can cause huge changes—positive and negative—in orders for manufacturing.

Medical companies have not tackled this problem with urgency in the past, but companies are more focused on it now and are aware they have to deal with this strategically. The large gross margins may have lulled the companies into not being as vigilant on pricing as the airlines in the past. However, with hospitals or health maintenance organizations (HMO) banding together to increase their purchasing power, the medical devices companies, too, have started paying more attention to pricing and pricing related processes.

Manufacturing

The manufacturing sector does not have the IT sophistication of the airlines industry or the big gross margins of the medical devices sector. Managers' focus is on engineering and production internally and on sales externally. This means that price and pricing processes do not get adequate attention. However, pressures on profit can push manufacturers to start looking at price carefully. Consider the example of a mid-sized industrial manufacturer.

This manufacturer, facing unprecedented inflation in their raw material costs, gathered a multifunctional team to figure out how to get a much needed price realization. The company had a history of regular price increases but seldom realized any price gains in transactions. The group brainstormed over a few days and came back with a long list of factors that affected price realization in the company. The following were some of the issues they discovered:

- Sales representatives had discount guidelines but often negotiated with customers without following the company's approval escalation process procedures. Once the customer agreed to a low price, their superiors or Pricing had no choice but to honor the price.
- The customer had paid less for a product in the past either because they were encouraged to try a new product, had bought the product as a substitute, or had received a one-time discount for some other reason. The original communication to the customer had not listed the exception or that the exceptional price was not a substitute for the regular price. The customer therefore was in a situation to demand the same price again in future transactions.
- The company had launched promotions at one time that had expiration dates, but some of the promotions had not been closed in the system, allowing various company personnel to use promotion codes that still generated the original discount.
- The quoting database system did not have correct prices for newly launched products. The prices for these products had to be manually "corrected" by one of the over 150 customer service personnel on calls with customers. The sheer workload, lack of knowledge regarding the value of the product, and relationships with Sales reps and even customers got in the way of consistently setting a

profitable price. It is easy to imagine that when a customer interfaced with two different customer service reps they not only felt entitled to the lower price but also questioned price levels of other products that had always been correct.

These problems are not unique to this company. Such problems typically linger on until a dire need or strong leader motivates the company to improve price-related processes.

2.3 Why Price Leaks Occur

Many direct reasons for price leaks exist, but at the root are issues of control and compensation. The complexity of processes, the multiple functions involved, and the convolution of price structures and contracts—with the resulting complexity of IT systems—all result in a situation where it is difficult to build controls. On the other hand, there is the issue of incentives or compensation offered to different personnel or functional groups.

As we observed before, sales are the lifeblood of any company, so everyone is interested in higher sales. However, in the absence of controls, this objective can hurt not only price but also revenues. A strong motivation to increase sales can perversely result in weakening existing controls or not putting in required controls. After all, controls require cost and effort that proponents of promotions or other sales initiatives may not take into account.

Three causes for why controls on prices are difficult to create or implement are (1) the number of functions, business lines, regions, and so on involved in pricing decisions, (2) complexity of prices and their implementation in IT systems, and (3) incentives for different personnel and their objectives. Let us examine each in detail.

Multiple Functions, Business Lines, and Regions

One reason pricing processes in a company are complex is that they involve almost everyone in the company, or at least that is what everyone in the company thinks:

Price-setting is a complex process that spans multiple departments (organizational breadth) and several management layers (organizational depth). The resulting interactions of departments and hierarchies are difficult to comprehend and predict in any field of organizational study, but even more so with regard to a critical marketing mix element such as pricing.[1]

"Everyone" means people from different functions, different business lines, and different regions. Then there is the customer who is at odds with the company in that he wants the lowest price but the company wants the highest. Within the company different groups have different views and incentives. This sets the stage for different pricing processes, depending on where the pricing function is located and to whom it reports. The nature of pricing processes also depends on which function controls the agenda—Pricing, Finance, Sales, or Marketing.

Pricing involves the customer whether it is a direct customer or an indirect customer (intermediary). It involves the customer-facing Sales group as well. Then there is Marketing, which itself is a large, diverse group including marketing communications, brand managers, product managers, and marketing managers. Moreover, the senior management invariably steps into the decision process to discuss a sale or a contract when the customer is a large buyer or even a potentially large buyer.

The IT function is involved as a support role because they create and/or maintain the enabling systems and reporting. The systems may be point systems that are homegrown or provided by specialized vendors or enterprisewide implementations of enterprise-resource planning (ERP) such as SAP or Oracle.

Also involved is the Pricing Administration group as well as a multifunction Pricing Strategy group. The clout and effectiveness of the pricing function depends on where the Pricing group is within Marketing, Sales, Finance, or Strategy or if it is a standalone group—and on whether or not it has a clear control role.

Many companies demarcate pricing strategy from tactics by having Marketing own the list price and having Sales own the discounts and therefore the net price to customer. Oversight or control of realized prices is the responsibility of the Pricing or Finance group. While this explains roles at a high level, most price-related actions generate emotion because roles and responsibilities remain unclear and are defined or re-defined in the what-who-when of the action plan. This emotion generates the need to compromise:

> ...*Managers must compromise in terms of all the marketing mix elements of their value offering. The nature of these compromises has a profound impact on the price-setting policies of the firm. Therefore, the nature of accommodation as regards price-setting is one of compromise in the form of departmental sub-optimization.*[2]

Even in companies that have more of a shared understanding of their pricing processes than other companies, complexity arises from people in different business lines or geographical regions working with different processes. This has implications when the customer is a global customer and gets a chance to complain about not getting the same price or discounts in all their markets.

Complexity of Prices and IT Systems

Adding to the complexity of pricing processes is complexity around "price" itself. Companies offer prices to customers as list prices based on quantity, discount structure (volume), rebates, promotions, spot pricing, and even multiproduct discounts that are based on the customer buying more than a threshold amount.

Then there are channel-specific processes: direct versus indirect sales (the former to customers and the latter to independent distributors or other intermediaries) and online and even mail-order or catalog sales to small customers. Terms and conditions involving payment schedule (discounts based on early payment) and freight add to the complexity of the price and hence to the pricing processes to ensure control and compliance.

Furthermore, how a company communicates the price to the customer adds another wrinkle: hard copy catalogs or price lists, web displays, email updates, or letters (and who communicates with whom in the customer company). Not updating prices in the system can also be a source for price leaks as customers can get older lower prices.

This means controls are not just difficult to enforce but also difficult to envision before an initiative gets under way. Certainly, IT-based controls are part of the solution, but given the complexity of processes and of prices, the IT system can itself become a source for price leaks as not all situations can be visualized when implementing controls.

Incentives and Pricing Objectives

Incentives factor in functional and individual agendas. In one company, salespeople may be compensated at a straight commission rate on revenues. In other companies, incentives may be based on a two tier-system based on a lower commission up to a certain threshold of price and a higher commission for prices higher than this threshold. However, such a structure can sometimes creates an incentive for sales-people to ask the company to lower the threshold as part of the price approval process on one hand and with the customer to increase the actual price as part of the sales process on the other hand.

If bonus or incentives are based on year-on-year growth, this too can have unintended consequences. In one company, we discovered a sales manager holding back sales personnel from making sales for the rest of the year. This was because he had met his own "growth target" for the current year, and increasing sales further would have only created a bigger base for year-on-year growth for the following year!

Some companies also provide incentives to Sales leadership based on total margin to improve realized prices. However, most companies find it difficult to determine the cost of individual products accurately, and because Sales personnel do not have direct control on manufacturing costs, margin-based incentives tend to be less popular than revenue-based ones.

The Marketing group and other people within the company may get their bonuses based on sales, so their emphasis is on "growing the market" to increase revenues rather than increasing total profits, which can result in price leaks as well. This can create the pressure to close transactions quickly, and any controls are viewed as impediments. If a customer demands a product quickly, the salesperson may oblige with a price that is too low or sometimes too high because due diligence was not maintained.

Besides incentives, different managers may have different objectives in regard to pricing, sometimes even within the same function. Increasing long-term profits is certainly a goal, but managers may have other goals pertaining to market share or volume. Regardless, short-term profits may suffer with price leaks in day-to-day transactions. The sad result is that the consequent losses in short-term profits add up and result in loss of long-term profits as well.

Consider a particular manufacturing company in the medical supplies industry.[3] A survey of product managers from this company produced interesting findings related to their objectives for setting list prices. The product managers scored the different objectives on a 1–5 scale (1 = not important, 5 = very important) and, on average, rated increasing or maintaining market share as their top priority in both the short and the long run. Increasing sales volume is the second next priority. Increasing gross profit and increasing or maintaining margins are much lower down the list (see Table 2-2). It is clear from the survey that increasing profits is not very important, at least for the product managers at this company. If this company is typical, can we really be sure that realized prices and profits will be the highest possible?

Table 2-2 Average Importance Ratings of Pricing Objectives by Product Managers in a Medical Supplies Company

	Pricing Objective	Short-Run (<1 yr)	Long-Run (5 yrs)
		Average Score	Average Score
1	Increase/maintain market share	4.43	4.57
2	Increase/maintain sales volume	4.33	4.43
3	Project high quality image	4.24	4.00
4	Match competitors	4.19	4.24
5	Increase/maintain gross profit	4.14	4.38
6	Maintain level of competition	4.00	4.01
7	Avoid price wars	3.52	3.67
8	Increase/maintain sales revenue	3.48	3.57
9	Maintain distributor support	3.38	3.19
10	Increase/maintain gross margin	3.33	3.43
11	Achieve rational price structure	3.19	3.24
12	Erect/maintain barriers to entry	3.18	3.29
13	Undercut competitors	2.95	3.10
14	Increase/maintain liquidity	2.77	2.81
15	Avoid government attention	2.76	3.00
16	Avoid customer complaints about "unfair" prices	2.67	2.71

(Source: Diamantopoulos and Mathews, 1995)

We should note that the close average scores between various objectives imply there may be no overriding factor when it comes to setting list prices. Moreover, these averages cover up the disparities among the product managers themselves. If you add in the views of Marketing, Sales, and Finance personnel, we may get an even muddier picture. Still, if increasing profits or margins were high on everyone's list, the corresponding objectives would have shown up high on the list of averages as well.

In this company, these objectives apply to the setting of list prices. If you include the steps and the personnel involved in getting from the list price to the realized price in actual transactions, you can be reasonably sure that you will have price leaks not only from the list prices being too low, but also from discounts in individual transactions because of the pressure to increase market share or sales volume.

2.4 The Role of the Pricing Function

Who "owns" pricing is a long-debated question. Companies have been trying to determine the best place for pricing as a function for some time. In most company environments, it would require a multilevel and multidepartmental organization to be able to price both competitively (using market-based pricing) and profitably (value-based pricing). However, the question remains about how a company rises above departmental incentives and silos to achieve this.

Many companies have a dedicated Pricing team to interact with multiple internal groups, including customer-facing teams, to establish price-related policies and action plans. Such a group provides guidance and analysis.

Control is an important role that the pricing function plays. Pricing can track exceptions to agreed-upon guidelines and contracts: The frequency and magnitude of such exceptions indicates how serious the pricing leaks are in a company. Traditional pricing roles also include reporting on realized prices in the past month or week. Where a company is global, the pricing function can help ensure consistency in pricing processes across geographical regions around the globe through standardized metrics. The same applies across business lines.

The responsibilities of the pricing function, however, can be broader than just "controlling" or policing realized prices. The Pricing group can help develop a pricing strategy to respond to competition or increased prices of raw materials or components. At least part of Pricing's value lies in providing analysis of past realized prices by slicing the data by customer, by location, by product category, and so on and understanding the implications of changing and of realizing prices.

The Pricing group can also provide input on new product pricing and weigh their experience of compliance challenges, regional differences, and competition along with product managers, Marketing, and Sales. Developing a price for a new product (or revising it for an existing one) is not just a matter of coming up with one number. As mentioned previously, it involves a rule-based discount structure—size of customers, seasonality, application, cost-to-serve, product type, product lifecycle, location, and so on—and the Pricing group can do that. The same can apply to promotions and special discounts that Marketing comes up with, and Pricing can provide the analysis to show the implications of such discounts.

The Pricing group can also help with understanding product differentiation in terms of price as well as price implications of having different channels of direct and indirect distribution. Evaluating contracts and terms of existing and proposed contracts is another role where Pricing can contribute to the company.

In most companies, however, there is a difference between what the role of Pricing is stated to be and what it actually is. Different groups and individuals are "involved" with pricing and have different incentives. Depending on the industry and company, these groups or individuals have differing amounts of sway. As such, Pricing's real role in a company can range from merely tracking prices proposed by sales representatives to actively participating in controlling and communicating prices in contract design and in strategic and operational pricing. Approaches such as Six Sigma Pricing can help streamline pricing processes and develop a clear role for all parties concerned to find ways that help maximize total profits in both the short and the long term.

Consider again the aforementioned manufacturer of medical supplies as an illustration of a process for creating and reviewing list prices.[4] Setting of list prices in this company was done once a year for all products, and the prices remained constant for the year. Introduction of new products resulted in price supplements. Distributors for this company's products were given a discount off the list price and were encouraged to sell at the marked list price but were not required to do so.

The price review took place every fall, and the process was mostly centralized within the Marketing department. The department priced two-thirds of the products based on their scores on three attributes in a pricing model that used laborious manual calculations. Half of the remaining products were initially priced this way, but then the product managers adjusted these prices based on their perception of market conditions. The remainder of the products were priced by product managers as they saw fit without using the pricing model.

Finance had sales and profit goals for the coming year, and meeting these required the Marketing department to adjust prices. The Finance department used a simple formula to compute a standard cost and hence the gross profit margin, given the discounted price, for each product. The formula was based on the number of stages required for each product's production, the cost of materials and labor for one unit of the product for each stage, and variable and fixed overheads for each stage used for each product. There was considerable interaction between the Marketing and the Finance departments before the company made price lists public.

A pricing function could be quite useful in this company, not for controlling discounts in this case, but for the annual process of setting and reviewing list prices. Despite there being a process that was repeated every year for many products, the process was still more-or-less ad hoc with pricing responsibility scattered across Marketing and Finance departments and product management in this company.

2.5 Summary

Inefficiency of pricing processes due to lack of effective controls results in loss of profits. As price is diluted in transactions, profits fall away in a variety of ways.

In one company, a focus group pointed to prices in transactions being unduly low because of a number of reasons such as customers demanding and getting yet another one-off discount because they got one in the last transaction, because they were able to use a quote from two years ago before two price hikes took effect, or because there were "special circumstances" that motivated the Sales rep to offer an extra-large discount to the customer without waiting for Pricing to approve the price. These may all be valid at the level of the individual transaction, but all such events leak profits.

These leaks happen because of the complexity of processes, the multiple functions involved, and the convolution of price structures and contracts and then the resulting complexity of IT systems. Then there is the issue of varying incentives of people from different functions. Moreover, there is no clear or overriding pricing objective in a company as we shall see in the case study in the next chapter.

3

CASE STUDY— PRICING OPERATIONS AND SIX SIGMA PRICING

Do not believe in anything simply because you have heard it...or because it is spoken and rumored by many...or because it is found written in your religious books...But after observation and analysis, when you find that anything agrees with reason and is conducive to the good and benefit of one and all, then accept it and live up to it.

—*The Buddha*

Chapter reprinted by permission of Harvard Business Review *from "Six Sigma Pricing" by ManMohan Sodhi and Navdeep Sodhi, May 2005.*

3.1 Introduction

Before getting into the specifics of Six Sigma Pricing, we describe the application of Six Sigma Pricing at a global manufacturer of industrial equipment we call "Acme" for reasons of confidentiality. We have taken this case study from our article, "Six Sigma Pricing," printed in the *Harvard Business Review* in May 2005 (reprinted with permission).

Acme applied Six Sigma rigorously to its price-setting process for one product line to great effect. The company met its target of increasing annual revenue by $500,000 in less than three months. When Acme subsequently raised list prices across the board, the company reaped the full value of the increase for this product line—but much less for others. In just six months, annual revenue increases reached an eye-popping $5.8 million for this product line alone, all of which went straight to the bottom line.

Not only did the reforms stem the revenue leaks, they also removed much of the organizational friction that had long bedeviled the company's pricing process by making it clear who had authority over which pricing decisions. Uncertainty about pricing policy (or rather the appearance of it) may help salespeople in their negotiations with customers, but it does a company no good for its own people to be confused and in conflict.

At Acme, that tension was readily apparent. On the one hand, Acme's sales reps saw their mission as building market share, which was senior management's stated aim. Being close to the customer, they felt they knew what the best price was. They saw the pricing managers and analysts as obstructions, out of touch, and too slow to respond to changing facts on the ground. They would often circumvent the necessary checks and controls on invoiced prices, sometimes eroding the company's profit margins.

On the other hand, the pricing analysts saw themselves as the guardians of Acme's profitability, providing essential pricing analysis and, in their opinion, quick turnaround on approvals. As we will see, the Six Sigma project generated hard evidence that significantly reduced the tension in this uneasy Sales–Pricing relationship, which became less influenced by gut instinct or emotion.

3.2 Background

The trigger for the project was a change in market conditions, which put Acme under considerable pricing pressure. The price of two key raw materials, steel and petroleum, had risen quickly and sharply, threatening to inflict a projected $20 million in unplanned annual incremental costs on the company. Some of its steel suppliers had even refused to honor existing contracts. Overall, average costs had doubled within the space of a few months.

The company had no choice but to raise list prices. But by how much? If Acme raised prices too much, it stood to lose customers to rivals. If it raised prices too little, it would not be worth the effort to announce and implement the change. Moreover, Acme could not be sure whether a nominal increase in list prices would even hit the bottom line. Acme's pricing processes made it difficult to control the price that was actually invoiced.

Acme's myriad products could each be configured in numerous ways, according to customers' needs, and the company published list prices for every possible configuration. But each sale then had its own individually approved discount and hence its own invoiced price. Prices and discounts were set by the Pricing division. Acme's Sales division had market-specific blanket ceilings for percentage discounts on all products, and Sales reps had to obtain authorization from Pricing to offer deeper discounts. Pricing either approved the request or set a slightly higher approved price, typically expressed as a percentage of the list price. After the transaction was completed, Sales invoiced the customer with a final transaction price, which was (in principle) the same as or slightly higher than the approved price.

But it was well known that top management frowned on losing market share, and the absence of any effective controls encouraged some sales-people to short-circuit the process. A Sales representative would ask Pricing for discounts that were much deeper than the guidelines allowed for, and even if Pricing complied, the representative might offer a further, unapproved discount to close a deal. For instance, one order approved by Pricing at $81,000 was actually invoiced at $75,000, and another at $31,000 was invoiced at $28,000.

With tens of thousands of sales transactions per year, the task of making sure each invoice accorded with the list and approved prices was daunting. But the lack of control over final prices meant that even if Acme could work out how much of a hike in list prices the market could bear, the company still could not be sure it would actually see the increase in each transaction or even overall across transactions.

3.3 Six Sigma

How to get a grip on the situation? Senior managers began by considering what other parts of the organization had done to bring similarly variable processes under control. They knew that Acme had enjoyed considerable success in reducing manufacturing variability by applying the famous Six Sigma discipline. Employees from different functions and organizational levels understood the methodology, and some had company-specific Six Sigma certification, holding titles such as "green belt" and "black belt," following the example of such companies as Motorola and General Electric.

It seemed to Acme's executives that pricing closely resembled many manufacturing processes. A product's invoiced price could be considered a final product, the result of a "manufacturing" process encompassing several stages. They decided, therefore, to pilot a Six Sigma Pricing project in one of the company's North American subsidiaries. If the project led to better control of final prices, they could roll out the approach throughout the company's entire global operations.

A manager from Pricing was appointed as project manager to carry out the five Six Sigma steps: define, measure, analyze, improve, and control.

He was given the help of a Six Sigma expert, or "Master Black Belt," recruited from the manufacturing side. The project sponsor was the senior executive responsible for pricing.

3.4 Define

Acme's project manager proposed that a defect should be defined as a transaction invoiced at a price lower than the one Pricing had approved (or lower than the current blanket guidelines when approval had not been sought). Note that defects are being defined in relative terms, according to the blanket floors set for the salespeople and the guidelines established by the pricing analysts. If the market were to take a turn for the worse, the floors and guidelines could be lowered; if the market were to strengthen, they could be raised. A defect occurs only when the actual invoiced price is out of compliance with the guidelines.

Once the definition of a defect was set, the project manager, with the help of the sponsor, recommended an appropriate scope for the project—that is, whether the project should be limited to only one particular product or applied to several product lines. In this case, the project sponsor limited the scope to one particular product line.

The next step for the project manager was to propose a charter for the project that specified the expected deliverables. Given the definition of a defective price, it was clear that this project would have to deliver the following:

• A better understanding of the existing pricing process.
• A modified process to control and, hence, improve final transaction prices.
• A way to track the improvement in realized prices and to monitor compliance with the modified process.

Next, to collect data, carry out analysis, and ensure everyone's buy-in for any subsequent implementation, the project manager enlisted people from the Pricing, Finance, Marketing, IT, and Sales divisions to be part of the Six Sigma team. The various members of the team were chosen for their functional and analytical expertise. The Finance person, for example, was chosen because she was familiar with the many pricing-related reports Acme was currently generating and with many of the company's data sources.

In addition, to endow the project with institutional backing and ensure that team members had good access to data, the project manager asked people in positions of influence at Acme to serve on a Steering Committee for the project. The chair of the committee was the project sponsor. Other members included the director of Sales, the vice president of IT, the vice president of Finance, and the vice president of Marketing. They agreed that the project manager would meet with the team and the steering committee as needed to keep them apprised of the project's progress.

The first duty of the team was to confirm the proposed problem definition and project charter and to set a financial goal for the project. That was no easy task, as it was the first time Acme had ever embarked on such a project. Nonetheless, the team set a goal of increasing revenue by $500,000 in the first year following implementation. This additional revenue was to come entirely from more efficient price management—in other words, from actions that did not incur any losses in market share or unit sales volumes. This was a far more ambitious number than Acme had ever set for comparably sized manufacturing or service Six Sigma projects, which had typically delivered average annual cost savings of less than $100,000.

3.5 Measure

At Acme, the project manager began by mapping the price agreement process, with team members helping to fill in process details. To generate and verify the information he needed, the project manager formally interviewed eight colleagues from five functional divisions: IT, Sales, Pricing, Finance, and Marketing. He also sought informal feedback from other people in these functions. As a result of this exercise, the team was able to draw a high-level diagram of the entire process showing the flow of information from one step to the next (see Figure 3-1).

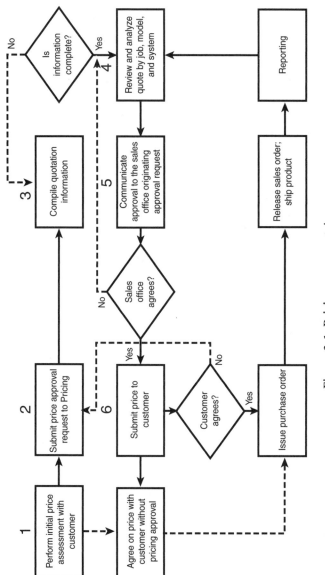

Figure 3-1 Pricing process at Acme

The map was supported by documentation detailing the inputs (called X's in Six Sigma parlance) and outputs (Y's) associated with each step, showing all the people and IT systems involved, and specifying whether the decision-making inputs could be controlled by Pricing or Sales. The eventual output variable for the entire process is the final transaction price, but intermediate steps have their own intermediate outputs. For example, after an initial discussion with a customer, the output could be an agreed-upon price that conforms to guidelines, or it might be a proposed price that would have to be referred to Pricing for approval. The inputs are the characteristics of the deal, such as the product type, order size, or time of year.

The map revealed a pricing process with six main steps. Although it seemed straightforward in principle, it was clear that in practice the sequence did not work smoothly, was replete with exceptions and shortcuts, and that the quality of inputs available to Sales or Pricing personnel in any step could be quite poor.

Step 1. Perform initial price assessment with customer (Sales).
The inputs for this are the list price, the blanket discount guidelines for Sales in the particular market, and the customer's product and pricing requirements. The output is a tentative price (that is, a discount off the list price). Approval is needed from Pricing if the discount is deeper than the maximum authorized for the particular market.

Step 2. Request pricing approval from Pricing (Sales).
For the Pricing personnel receiving such a request, the inputs are the price the Sales rep has requested and the guidelines for pricing analysts. In practice, sometimes this step, and most of the subsequent ones, were circumvented when a Sales rep offered a final discounted price to the customer without prior Pricing approval.

Step 3. Compile quotation information (Pricing).
The input is the information about the customer and the order provided by the sales rep to support his or her request. The output is the complete details of the transaction in question. This step should be trivial but often, in practice, the Sales rep did not or could not provide enough information about

the quotation, and the Pricing analyst or manager would have to chase around to get the missing information.

Step 4. Review and analyze quote (Pricing).
Inputs are the completed quotation information generated in the previous steps, including the tentative price the Sales rep has requested, reports summarizing the history of similar transactions in the particular market and, when available, reports of similar transactions with the same customer. In theory, such reports would guide Pricing's efforts to accept or modify the price requested and to produce the output—the tentative approved price. In reality, with information scattered in different computer systems, the guidelines available to the Pricing analyst could be quite poor. Or the Sales rep might request a very quick turnaround, leaving little time for a Pricing analyst to carry out this step effectively.

Step 5. Communicate approval to Sales office (Pricing).
The input is the tentative approved price from the analysis in the previous step and any additional information regarding the order and customer. The output is the approved price. This should be the penultimate step before the Sales rep approaches the customer but, in practice, this could instead be the beginning of a prolonged negotiation between Sales and Pricing. Other people might weigh in at this point as well, and the final approved price could end up quite a bit lower because of pressure from a manager or from a more senior sales or marketing executive.

Step 6. Submit price to customer (Sales).
The input is the approved price. The output is the tentative price for invoicing that the Sales rep submits to the customer. At this point, the Sales rep should simply be offering the customer the approved price. But this entire project was based on the observation that the price that the Sales rep actually offered to the customer, as indicated by the invoices from the subsequent transaction (if there were one), could be quite a bit lower than the approved price.

Before moving on to the next stage of the project, the team assessed the quality of the input data that supported the pricing process. It would be difficult to improve the process if the current steps systematically produced faulty data. Moreover, the team needed to have faith in the numbers on which it was going to base its findings and recommendations. By examining representative samples of data in detail, the team was able to confirm that the actual sales transaction data were by and large stable and reliable, even though different reports presented the information in different formats.

3.6 Analysis

To aid in their analysis, the Acme team used a common Six Sigma tool called the cause and effect (C&E) matrix to guide discussion. With the help of the Master Black Belt, the project manager held a workshop using the tool to identify problems and put them in order of priority. The rows on the C&E matrix list all the steps in the current process, and the columns list all of the requirements that the customers of each step in the process have, each weighted according to how important each requirement is to the customer. For the Acme team, the "customers" were senior executives who wanted better controls in, and eventually better price performance from, the pricing process.

The team did not actually assign number scores. Instead, members used the structure of the matrix to focus on possible causes for lack of control at each step. The process diagram was projected as a slide, and team members used a whiteboard to discuss each step in turn. The main findings from this exercise suggested that the defects arose largely from problems in Steps 1, 4, and 6 and from failures in reporting:

Step 1: The team found that the ability of the Sales reps to help customers select the right products and the right features for those products was critical to managing customers' price expectations. Unfortunately, salespeople's failures in assessing customer requirements could not be easily detected and controlled.

Step 4: The key constraint here was time; Sales reps sometimes wanted discount approval within hours of forwarding a request, which made it difficult for pricing analysts to work out whether or not the discount was reasonable. Giving Pricing more time for analysis would make it easier to reduce the incidence of defective pricing.

Step 6: Sales reps sometimes offered final prices to customers without prior approval, leaving Pricing with little choice but to OK the price after the fact. The team agreed that such situations should be tracked.

Reporting

Information about transactions was not gathered or presented in a consistent manner. The unit's various functions generated more than a hundred different transaction reports that summarized sales data by product line, market, and other ways at weekly, monthly, or quarterly intervals. Discrepancies and redundancies in those reports led to variability in the decisions analysts came to in deciding prices. This meant that managers could neither track pricing defects easily nor obtain the data they needed in time to do adequate due diligence on price quotes (Step 4).

After completing the C&E workshop, the project manager did a standard statistical analysis of transaction-level data for all of the individual transactions that occurred in the two years before the project started. He discovered that actual transaction prices were distributed along a normal bell-shaped curve around the average transaction price, demonstrating the classic problem Six Sigma targets—that the high rates of defects (in this instance lower-than-approved prices) stem from high variability. What's more, the price range for transactions of different sizes overlapped significantly, suggesting that pricing guidelines were not differentiated enough for different-sized transactions. If the Six Sigma team could reduce the variability of transaction prices, it would address both problems.

In addition, the analysis revealed that salespeople serving certain territories within the same market had a greater tendency than their colleagues in other territories to invoice at prices either significantly higher or lower than approved. The team concluded from this analysis that different pricing guidelines needed to be set not only for different transaction sizes but also for different territories within the same market and possibly even for customer groups. Pricing guidelines had always been market-specific but were not differentiated by transaction sizes, territories, or, for the most part, by customer group.

3.7 Improvement

The results from the analysis created a lot of positive buzz among Acme's senior managers. It was time to recommend modifications to the existing process to decrease the number of unapproved prices without creating an onerous approval process. Response speed was critical for salespeople so that they could continue to act quickly and close deals. But this was a challenge for Pricing personnel. What they needed, the team concluded, was clear guidelines to help them decide when they should or should not approve any deeper-than-usual discounts that Sales had requested or promised to customers.

The team proposed giving graduated discount approval authority to individuals in three levels of the organization's hierarchy: Sales reps or managers, pricing analysts, and the pricing manager. Finally, at a fourth level, top executives could continue to approve discounts without any limit. For example, in one particular market for a transaction size between $100,000 and $150,000, a Sales representative could offer any discount up to 30%, but to be able to offer an even lower price to a customer, he would have to contact a pricing analyst for approval. She would first check against the guideline price for that region, type of product, transaction size, and perhaps other criteria, and use this to negotiate with the Sales rep any further discount, up to 35%. If the Sales rep felt that the situation demanded an even lower price than the analyst could authorize, the request would be elevated to the pricing manager, who could approve a discount of up to 40%. If the salesperson was going for an even lower price, the request was passed up to a specified group at the top leadership level, which alone could approve a higher discount. Making both the guidelines and the escalation process clear speeded up the process by making it more efficient.

In cases where Sales representatives had already offered a customer a price and needed post-hoc authorization, the new process required that the rep involve his boss, who would have to e-mail or call Pricing for approval. The price already offered would still be honored, but now reps could be held more accountable for making unauthorized commitments.

The new distribution of pricing responsibilities required a process for developing—and, from time to time, reevaluating—all of the discount limits. To ensure that limits did not become outdated, the team created a spreadsheet tool that let Pricing work off recent transaction history.

The team also created exception codes that enabled Acme to track the reasons for variations in prices. The codes made it clear who had been involved in the decision to deviate from guidelines. For instance, if someone from leadership had approved a deep discount, the eventual transaction was tagged with a Leadership Approval code. If Acme needed to match a competitor's aggressive price, the pricing manager could approve a low price that was tagged with a Competitive Match code. If a Sales rep had already promised a price to a customer before getting approval, the transaction would have to be tagged with a Sales Error code. Pricing would now have 24 hours to do due diligence before approving a price request, and Acme tracked which Sales reps consistently asked for extra-fast turnarounds.

3.8 Control

Acme set up a monthly review at which executives—mainly the vice presidents of Marketing, Sales, and Finance, along with their direct reports—look at the company's overall performance and at particular geographic markets and transaction sizes to see if the new process is indeed resulting in higher average transaction prices, fewer exceptions, and no loss in market share. If prices are under control but the company is losing market share, it might be a sign that Acme needs to review pricing guidelines or take a look at how Sales reps are managing their territories. If the review group notices that a particular Sales rep is frequently making Sales Error transactions, the rep's boss will take a closer look at how the rep is negotiating. And, if the review group sees that transactions of a particular size regularly require the pricing manager's approval, the group instigates a reexamination of the pricing guidelines for that transaction size.

3.9 Results

The initial goal of generating $500,000 in incremental revenues in the first year was handily exceeded in only three months. More important, following a subsequent across-the-board list price increase, the average transaction price for the pilot product went up by slightly more than the percentage increase in list prices. In other words, the list price increase fully reflected in the top line for this product. By contrast, other product lines realized less than half the increase. That list price increase, together with the tighter controls the Six Sigma team developed and implemented, resulted in the $5.8 million in incremental sales in just the first six months following implementation, all going straight to the bottom line.

From an organizational perspective, the Six Sigma approach has considerably reduced the friction inherent in the Sales–Pricing relationship. The exercise of systematically collecting and analyzing price transaction data gave pricing analysts hard evidence to counter the more intuitively based claims that the sales staff had typically advanced in negotiating discounts. A frequent claim, for instance, was that "My customers want just as high a percentage discount for a $3,000 transaction as they would get for a $300,000 one." Now that Pricing knows that Acme's customers tend to accept lower discounts on smaller transactions than on bigger ones and that some customers are willing to pay higher prices than others, analysts can more easily push back when negotiating price approvals with Sales staff. They can respond confidently and authoritatively when Sales reps ask questions such as, "Why is my authorized price higher than those in another market?" or "How come we don't authorize the same price for all customers?"

Salespeople, for their part, are less likely to feel that the negotiation with Pricing is driven by political motives or by purely personal desires to assert control. Moreover, they can use the same data to press their own points. It became clear, for example, that some Sales offices that had previously been under scrutiny for aggressive pricing practices had in fact been acting perfectly reasonably given their local market conditions.

In light of the project's success and its low cost, Acme is rolling out Six Sigma pricing across the entire organization. Other companies operating in competitive environments can also benefit from Acme's experience as they look for ways to exercise price control without alienating customers. They can transform the tenor of the relationship between their Pricing and Sales staffs from adversity to relative harmony by giving them a process for making joint decisions that are aligned with company objectives and based on solid data and analysis.

3.10 Summary

Although the name is fictitious, Acme is a real global manufacturer of industrial equipment that found itself caught between rising steel and petroleum prices on one hand and being unable to raise prices effectively to pass on cost increases to its customers. Although it could raise list prices, there was no guarantee that under the highly varying discount levels on individual transactions, there would be any effective price increase. They decided to tackle the problem of discounts being too high first, as these affected the bottom line directly.

Just as manufacturing processes can sometimes produce defects, Acme noted that the pricing process, entailing their Sales and Pricing personnel, occasionally produced unacceptably low realized prices (that is, unacceptably high discounts). Acme had successfully used Six Sigma to reduce defects with its manufacturing processes so it felt it could take the same approach with pricing processes.

Acme then conducted the five steps of the Six Sigma method on the pricing process for a particular division of products in North America, which are

- (D) **Define:** To define the problem of excessive discounts on individual transactions
- (M) **Measure:** To describe the processes and to collect the data associated with transactions over the previous 12 months

- **(A) Analyze:** To brainstorm on which steps of the process to focus on and to use statistical tools to study the spread of discount levels by region, by transaction size, and so on
- **(I) Improve:** To make recommendations on process changes
- **(C) Control:** To set up controls by way of monitoring when excessive discounts are given and to set up monthly review meetings to monitor the average discount levels as well as reasons for excessive discounts

By applying Six Sigma to their pricing process in just one division, Acme obtained $5.8 million in incremental profits in the first six months following implementation. Moreover, tension between Pricing and Sales reduced as the entire process and intermediate outcomes became more transparent to both sides.

The success of this project prompted us to advocate specializing Six Sigma to the area of pricing as Six Sigma Pricing, the subject of this book.

Part II

Basics—Pricing Operations and Six Sigma

4

PRICE AND PRICING

*Pricing is the moment of truth—all of marketing
comes to focus in the pricing decision.*

—Raymond Corey

4.1 Introduction

There are many price-related processes affecting or being executed by different people within a company. Stakeholders within a company may not have a complete view, a shared understanding, or a common sense of the purpose of all processes. For instance, even if the purpose of the process is understood well, some of the control-oriented steps may be perceived as "bureaucratic" procedures without bottom-line benefit and therefore as impediments to work around creatively.

We need to understand the different levels at which decisions are made. The focus of this book is not on pricing strategy at the boardroom level but on the process level for handling contracts and individual transactions. The context is primarily B2B with companies being from any of a broad variety of industries.

Any pricing process can have many stakeholders within the company. Consider, for example, list-price setting for a particular product (or service). This product may belong to a particular brand that is managed by a brand manager. It needs to be discounted for a particular customer who is "owned" by a Sales region or practice. It may be sold by the indirect or direct channel, so there are different channel managers. Finally, the product may be sold with or without a contractual agreement, with possibility of commission payoff to an integrator or other middleman, followed by possible sales growth-related rebates.

The stakeholders and many inter-related processes are expected to deliver the right product at the right price to the right customer at the right time. These pricing processes have different owners from different functions following different functional mandates, so coordination of efforts is not as good as it should be. One outcome of not coordinating these processes is inefficiency that takes the form of price dilution and hence, profit leaks.

4.2 Different Types of Prices

Pricing processes exist in different contexts, and the very notion of "price" may mean different things to different people within the same company. One reason is that there are prices at many different levels for any item—even for a specific transaction. For simplicity, we categorize the various levels of price as (1) *list price*, (2) *actual or realized price*, and (3) *approved or system-generated price*.

List Price

The *list price* is the published price. Depending on the industry, country of origin, or B2B versus B2C, it may be called the sticker price, manufacturer's suggested retail price (MSRP), or the recommended retail price (RRP). Companies use the list price as the base for any discounts to customers in B2B transactions.

Setting list prices is a strategic decision depending on multiple factors such as minimum margin requirement, competitive price and product value offering, as well as the desired market positioning of the product. At the time of a product's launch, we can think of the initial list price as the "new product price." During the lifecycle of this product, the list prices may be adjusted to make room for newer products launched by the company or its competitors, keeping the product relevant to changes in a company's direction and the customer needs. Companies also need to change list prices when the cost of raw materials or other inputs go above the level at which their cost structure would allow the company to absorb.

Sometimes a company may publish list prices by unit volume. Other companies maintain separate list prices for different categories of customers that could be based on volume of sales or on the particular situation of the customer or the customer segment.

In some industries, companies continually introduce new products to maintain list prices averaged across their products high or to go after previously untapped markets. Consider, for instance, the medical device industry. Companies in this industry innovate and upgrade products through Research and Development (R&D). They seek to generate the highest return on their R&D and other investment by setting list prices of new products at the highest possible level within the constraints of government regulation and their competitive price envelope. They also reset list prices of their existing product portfolio to retain customers not enthralled by new technology, while using the new products to satisfy those awaiting the latest innovation. This way, companies can protect market share and still penetrate new customer segments. They also launch new products with fewer features and lower list prices to go after untapped customer segments with less purchasing power than the existing customer base.

Besides setting list prices, companies occasionally seek to increase their list prices for at least two reasons: First, raw material costs may increase, or the government may impose new regulation that increases compliance cost for the company's industry. All companies in this industry then have to rely on price increases to protect profits. Second, industry demand may increase making it difficult to service customers at current levels of capacity. This leads companies to raise prices and/or add capacity to meet the market opportunity.

The list price increase may not be reflected in the realized prices depending on customer acceptance and competitors' willingness to comply with a new "going rate." The Goodyear Tire and Rubber Company raised prices of tires in February, June, and September of 2005 due to surging oil prices. From Goodyear's perspective, a $1 increase in the cost per barrel of petroleum meant $20 million in incremental manufacturing costs, so it had to increase list prices. The price increase in 2005 of 5–8% meant that a distributor should sell a tire originally selling for $100 for as much as $108. However, customers would have balked at buying Goodyear tires at higher prices if its competitors chose not to raise prices. Consequently, Goodyear distributors may continue to sell tires at the old price to match or beat competition. This would mean that Goodyear would have to increase discounts for these distributors and would not realize the incremental price despite the list price increase.

Thus, announcing the list price increase is easier than actually realizing increased prices from customers. For this reason, companies generally refrain from increasing list prices.[1]

Actual or Realized Price

The *net price* is the amount on the invoice that the customer has agreed to pay the company in a specific transaction. There may be further discounts that apply, say at year-end, based on total volume in the past year.

Different companies use different terms to describe what they eventually get from the customer. Aside from the discount at the transaction level, there may be many factors that go into the realization of this "net price." Starting from the list price, a company might apply the following discounts or rebates for a particular customer to get the realized price for the transaction (see Figure 4-1):

- A contract discount on the specific transaction if a pertinent contract is in place
- A volume-based discount depending on dollar size of transaction or quantity of items purchased
- A rebate based on last year's total sales
- A rebate based on incremental sales in the coming year

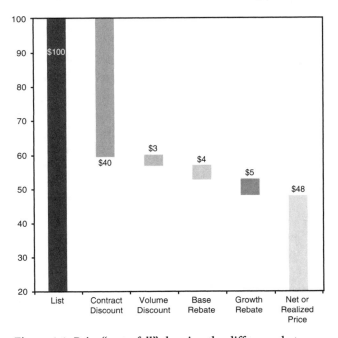

Figure 4-1 Price "waterfall" showing the difference between the list price and the realized price

Determining the discount to offer a customer is a pricing process. In the absence of suitable controls, these processes may leak prices and hence revenue despite the existence of clear guidelines in regard to the level of these discounts and the circumstances in which any particular customer or category of customers get a particular level.

With different functions having their own incentives and goals, different interpretations of the guidelines as well as the purpose of developing those guidelines exist. Companies that study past invoices are usually surprised to find how much of their business is not compliant with set guidelines or contract terms. Recall the medical devices company mentioned earlier that estimated their annual loss of profits to be $60 million by not ensuring compliance from customers regarding the terms and conditions in their contracts.

System-Generated or Approved Price

The bridge between the list price and the actual price paid by customers is, or should be, the system-generated or approved price. The system-generated price reflects an administrative process ensuring controls to approve discounts. These discounts may apply to a product category, to a customer contract, or to an individual transaction. In such a process, a controlling function within the company, generally Pricing, inputs the maximum allowable discounts and rebates for a Sales or customer service representative involved in a particular transaction or type of transaction. Moreover, the company may allow for additional discounts based on certain conditions such as size of a transaction or a promotional price.

Ideally, the controlling division, typically Pricing, takes into account any existing contract terms and conditions, the market situation, product inventory, and input from Sales (or Customer Service) to estimate the smallest possible discount that would ensure a sale. If the process is working, the actual price should be the same as or slightly less than the approved price.

In practical terms, however, controls to enforce the approved price may be weak or missing even if an approval process is in place and the actual prices may be above or below the approved price. Moreover, the approval process needs controls to ensure that the system-generated prices are in alignment with existing company policies. After all, system-generated prices are the output of the approval process, and if this process does not follow pricing guidelines, neither will system prices or actual prices. A direct implication is that if approval processes do not keep up with the changes in list price, a company may be unable to extract the same percentage increase from customers.

4.3 Different Levels of Pricing

Prices are set at different levels in a company, and we need to differentiate between these levels to ensure clarity around what we mean by "pricing" when we talk about Six Sigma Pricing. At one level is pricing strategy that is concerned with the *positioning* of the company's products in the price spectrum in the market alongside competitors' products. At a different level is setting the discount off the list price for a specific transaction with a particular customer. There are different processes at and between these two levels.

For a number of reasons, pricing decisions are becoming increasingly tactical and operational rather than strategic.[2] Correspondingly, the importance of pricing is shifting from strategic and marketing-oriented pricing to operational and sales-oriented pricing. In this section, we discuss how strategic and operational pricing are different (See Table 4-1).

Table 4-1 Pricing at Three Levels

Pricing Level		Organizational Level	Frequency of Review/ Decision-Making
Strategic		Senior management	Annual (Quarterly, sometimes)
Operational	Tactical planning	Middle management	Monthly/Quarterly
	Execution	Customer service representatives; pricing analysts; middle management	Daily (or continually)

At the strategic level, the senior leadership in a company may desire to grow sales or market share to a certain level, to improve profitability to a stretch goal, to change the company's global footprint, or to achieve a position in the market as the high price-high-quality leader. These strategies typically have a decision horizon of a few years and are subject to change. For instance, from 2003 to 2006, Samsung Electronics strove to provide mobile phones at the top end of price, design, and quality. In contrast, from 2006 to 2007 the company revised its strategy to cater to the low end consumer as well to expand in India and China like its competitor Nokia.

These strategies engender, or at least should engender, tactical goals for the medium- and short-term over a few months to a year. These goals require multiple functions to work with one another and hence create many projects and workflows within each function. The Pricing function may lead or may just participate as an enabler in these projects.

On a day-to-day or weekly basis, the execution of transactions and contracts is or should be guided by the goals for the medium- and short-term. Execution involves Sales, IT, Marketing, and Legal personnel, among others who carry out specific steps or tasks critical for success.

The key point is that these three levels of pricing are, or should be, organizationally hierarchical. Decisions at one level should guide those at lower levels and in turn be supported and informed by their outcomes. Success eventually lies in execution, so flaws in execution or operational workflows will limit the success of even a good strategy. In the reverse direction, the absence of a strategy or having a poor inherent strategy in place will limit the results of successful execution regarding the bottom line.

When thinking about these levels, it would be helpful to keep in mind that Six Sigma Pricing is about improving repeatable and repeated processes. A pricing process that will be repeated many times a year must be solid in order to avoid repeating pricing or other defects throughout the course of the year. If a company has new products coming out once in a blue moon, Six Sigma Pricing is not relevant for improving the boardroom decision-making process of positioning these products in the marketplace. However, if the company comes up with new incremental products many times during a year, their pricing is a repeated process that can and should be standardized using Six Sigma Pricing.

Pricing Strategy

Pricing strategy refers to a company making a choice of positioning itself with respect to their competitors within the industry: high-price/high-value differentiation or low-price/low-value differentiation at the extremes. For instance, a company may choose a high-price/high-quality position. Companies also decide on brand image, target segment, and distribution channels to help maximize market penetration and profitable growth.

Once a company has made such choices, the next step of setting the price becomes easier. Alternatively, a company may choose to go after a mass market with a particular end consumer price in mind and then design the product and services to ensure a decent return-on-investment. A company does not make such long-term choices everyday.

Business textbooks refer to this level as "pricing," confusing this level with operational pricing processes. Strategic pricing is market-facing for the most part, requiring decision makers to study the market and its likely evolution in the months and years to come.

Six Sigma Pricing is not for creating pricing strategy and is not applicable at this level. However, Six Sigma Pricing can help to run operations to support the chosen pricing strategy more effectively. Moreover, the ability to run pricing (or any) operations tightly is a strategic advantage, so whether or not to use Six Sigma Pricing is a strategic decision.

Pricing Operations

Pricing operations entail two types of processes to ensure operationalizing and adhering to pricing strategy. These are

1. **Modification processes** involving list modifications in response to changes in the market environment (but not changes to strategy). For instance, increased petroleum prices in 2005

caused airlines to tag special fees as a way to increase list prices: such decisions are operational because they have a decision horizon of a few months at the most. Modifying price guidelines is also an operational process. Similarly, pricing of products in the same family at a company that produces more than a few of these every year is also operational. Communicating the list price changes in regard to customers and internal operations (such as ensuring the update of ERP or other systems) is also part of such operations.

2. **Control processes** to ensure and track adherence to price guidelines. The purpose of these processes is to ensure high levels of realized prices relative to list prices, the latter being the embodiment of pricing strategy. Control processes can also track whether a price promotion was effective in getting the hoped-for incremental sales and additional profits.

List price changes are not as frequent as individual transactions. Still, tighter operational processes make this process of modifying list prices easier. Tighter processes also ensure that once list prices are changed, these list price changes are implemented in the tens of thousands of transactions that follow.

Pricing operations and their embedded processes face both the world outside and inside the company. Like pricing strategy, pricing operations face the market. However, unlike strategy, operations work closely with internal processes that deal with the execution of transactions. For example, pricing operations entail observing changes in the market— say, the entry of Chinese companies like Haier in the household appliance market or sharp increases in supply costs like that of oil in 2005–2006. Pricing operations also translate these external changes to more restrictive or more lenient discounting guidelines as well as ensure adherence to these updated guidelines.

Six Sigma Pricing is applicable at this level as these are repeated processes. In reality, in any given company these processes may run in an ad hoc, on-off manner despite being repeated. Indeed, the more ad hoc operational processes, the greater the benefits the company can get from standardizing these processes by applying Six Sigma Pricing.

Whether market-facing or internally-focused, these processes require all levels of people in Marketing, Sales, Finance, Customer Service, IT, Inventory Management, and Legal to work together to produce intended results in executing strategy. Most of the steps for processes at this level are internal to the company and therefore under the company's control.

Execution at the Transaction Level

Execution refers to processes that result in the price that the customer accepts. The decision horizon here is localized to the transaction itself, although a discount that is too low or too high can have unintended long-term effects. The processes at this level are repeated many times each day, every day of the week, and every week of the year, resulting in tens of thousands of completed transactions a year. Indeed…

For a majority of companies, the management of transaction pricing is the most detailed, time-consuming, systems-intensive and energy-intensive task involved in gaining a price advantage.[3]

Therefore execution processes, like transaction pricing, should be streamlined, standardized, and brought under control. However, the reality in many companies is quite the opposite. Different incentives and not having a shared sense of "ownership" of the process across individuals and across functions result in execution that is anything but standard or in control.

A midsized multinational company may have over 1,000 Sales representatives and managers, over 300 customer service personnel, and up to 50 account representatives to work with 50 product managers and 15 pricing personnel. All these people have different functional incentives and different individual pressures. Not accounting for multiple currencies in global transactions and varying levels of market sophistication, a slight error in pricing a product for a customer at one of its sites could cause customer dissatisfaction. Customer Service and Sales may have to remedy the situation by offering the customer additional discounts. Such discounts hurt the profitability of not only the current transaction, but also future transactions with this customer and possibly others.

A company can use Six Sigma Pricing to control the processes at this level to reduce the percentage discount levels and price variations. There is an "upward" benefit: With these execution-level processes in control, the link from strategy to execution through operations is quite tight. Six Sigma Pricing can close the gap between lack of control and the extent of control that is desirable. Therefore, we not only ensure compatibility between the actual and the approved price but also ensure that the list price and any list-price increases are incorporated in the approved or system generated price.

Referring back to the Acme case study (Chapter 3), a transaction-level concession process may be as follows with personnel from either Sales or Pricing carrying out each step:

Step 1: Perform initial price assessment with customer (Sales).

Step 2: Request pricing approval from Pricing (Sales).

Step 3: Compile quotation information (Pricing).

Step 4: Review and analyze quote (Pricing).

Step 5: Communicate approval to Sales office (Pricing).

Step 6: Submit price to customer (Sales).

4.4 Summary

Price is not just a single number that appears at the end of a simple workflow, involving only two or three people. We need to understand that when we say "price," we can mean any of a few different types of prices—list price, system-generated or approved price, and invoice or realized price.

Pricing is complex as well. All functions manage pricing at a strategic or operational level. Pricing strategy is outward looking and refers to the company's choice of positioning itself with respect to their competitors; for instance, high-price/high-quality or low-price/low-quality. Pricing operations involve modification processes involving list price changes and control processes to ensure adherence to price guidelines. Execution at the transaction level refers to processes that result in the actual price that the customer accepts. However, different incentives and not having a shared understanding of who "owns" what part of a process results in execution that is anything but standard or in control.

Six Sigma Pricing is not for designing or choosing pricing strategies. However, having tighter processes at the operational and transaction levels leads to greater success in implementing the chosen pricing strategy.

5

PRICING OPERATIONS

The leader has to be practical and a realist, yet must talk the language of the visionary and the idealist.

—*Eric Hoffer (1902–1983)*

5.1 Introduction

Broadly speaking, there are two types of processes to ensure that pricing operations adhere to pricing strategy. These are: (1) processes involving list price changes and (2) processes to ensure adherence to pricing guidelines. The actual processes vary by industry or company depending on expertise of those involved and complexity of the strategy. Whether market-facing or internally-focused, these processes require people from Marketing, Sales, Finance, Customer Service, IT, Inventory Management, and Legal to work together in executing the strategy.

5.2 Processes and Roles

There are at least two main categories of processes:

1. **Processes involving list price changes**: These include, for instance, processes to adhere to the product lifecycle from the time the company launches the product to the time it phases out this product. Changes in the market environment (for example, inflation in copper and steel costs in 2004) may also require a company to respond through list price changes.

2. **Processes to ensure adherence to price guidelines**: These processes aim at ensuring that sales have consistently high levels of price realization. These processes may also track price-related promotions and other initiatives to check if they were effective in increasing revenues and profits despite lower margins.

There are many roles and functions involved with these processes in most companies (see Figure 5-1). The important thing to note is that strategic actions invariably require operations support. Their success depends on processes that get less attention overall and certainly less of the senior management mind share, despite their importance. The strategic action of changing list price is more successful when operational processes to implement strategy run tightly than when they run in an ad hoc fashion.

Consider three actions: list price increase, new product launch pricing, and price promotions. These depend heavily on operational-level processes. These processes pertain to (1) analysis and tracking, (2) discounting, and (3) price review. Not all three get senior managers' attention except when the situation is dire. Yet another example is communicating the list price changes to customers and to internal operations updating the ERP or other transactional systems.

Pricing Process/Stakeholder	Strategic (S) or Operational (O)?	Divisional Head	Brand Director	Finance Manager/Analyst	Director Marketing	Marketing Communications	Legal	Global Account Manager	Sales Representative	Customer Service Manager/Rep	Product Manager	Sales VP/Director	Country/Territory Manager	IT Manager/Analyst	Sales Manager	Pricing Director	National Pricing/Contacts Manager	Pricing/Contracts Analyst
Standard List Price Change	S & O	■		■	■	■		■	■	■	■	■	■	■	■	■	■	■
Price Promotions	O				■	■		■	■	■	■	■	■	■	■	■	■	■
Price Communication to Customers	O			■	■	■	■	■	■	■		■			■	■	■	■
New Product Launch Pricing	S & O	■			■			■		■	■		■	■	■	■	■	■
Multi-brand Pricing	S & O		■		■						■	■	■	■	■	■	■	■
Market Segment Pricing	S & O			■			■			■	■	■	■	■	■	■	■	■
Custom Product Pricing	O			■				■	■	■	■	■		■		■	■	■
Volume Incentive Programs and Rebates	O	■				■	■	■		■	■			■	■	■	■	
Multi-channel Pricing	S & O	■			■					■	■	■	■	■	■	■	■	
Global Contracts	S & O	■				■	■			■	■	■	■	■	■	■	■	
National or Regional Contracts	O				■	■		■			■	■	■	■	■	■	■	
Competitive Transactional Pricing Intelligence	O							■	■	■	■		■		■	■	■	■
Analysis, Tracking, and Reporting	O			■								■	■	■	■	■	■	■
Product Lifecycle Pricing	S & O							■	■		■		■		■	■	■	■
Discounts and Concessions Approval	O						■	■		■			■			■	■	■
Scorecards and Price Reviews	O			■									■			■	■	■

Figure 5-1 Typical roles in various processes

One way to distinguish "strategic" from "operational" processes or actions is to consider the frequency and decision horizon so what may be a strategic action in one company may well be an operational process in another. Companies carry out operational processes more frequently than they make price-related strategic actions. Operational decisions have a time horizon of only a few months at the most: For instance, increased petroleum prices in 2005 caused airlines to tack on special fees as a way to increase list prices as a temporary measure. Similarly, pricing products in the same family at a company that produces more than a few of these every year is operational.

The challenge for conscientious managers is how to bring to the attention of the broader organization that small amounts of dollars leaked from thousands of individual transactions inevitably add up to losing millions in profits. If you take care of the pennies in operations, you take care of pounds, euros and dollars in the company-wide bottom line. To illustrate this point, let us consider in detail some strategic actions and their dependence on pricing operations.

5.3 List Price Increase

Although changing the list prices in many companies is a strategic decision involving considerations of the competition and market conditions, implementing these changes is part of pricing operations.

Depending on their size and sophistication, companies invest great effort (sometimes in a coherent manner, sometimes not), involving many steps:

1. Start with a mandate for list price adjustment.

2. Apply intended price changes at various levels of product hierarchy.

3. Model desired changes at product family and SKU level.

4. Analyze impact on product families, customer segments, and channels.

5. Get support from Sales leadership and elicit feedback on the company's competitive stance and the customer's comfort level.

6. Generate detailed spreadsheets to enable IT to populate ERP databases with the new list prices.

7. Test procedures before making the price increase "live."

8. Inform customers of price changes in advance of an effective date; proactively negotiate with special customers.

9. Set up trouble-shooting in the price approval escalation process in case of exceptions.

10. Design special handling procedures for delivering price exceptions without causing process breakdowns.

11. Switch on new list prices and start tracking results in terms of realized price, profit (margins), and revenue.

Companies go through a list-price-change process typically in an annual cycle, but not all companies do it right each time. We have heard many complaints from pricing professionals from different companies:

- "They don't develop a detailed project plan and seem to rush into these things after a senior manager decides it is the right time."
- "The leadership does not understand the complexity of pricing procedures in our systems. The people who really understand the details are not included in the planning process."
- "The customer database was not updated, and it is not my fault if 1,300 customers did not receive the price increase communication."
- "We will not get much out of this increase because Sales has asked us to exclude a whole bunch of major customers already."

Many of these process problems can be resolved by clearly defining the scope and charging qualified owners with clear roles and responsibilities for the overall project and for the various steps of the project. A company could choose among any of the quality methodologies. In this book, we show how to achieve process control with Six Sigma, given its consensus building tools based on data and facts rather than on "gut feel" and "experience."

5.4 New Product Launch Pricing and Lifecycle Maintenance

The purpose of developing a new product is to fulfill an unmet customer need. Depending on their pricing expertise, a large number of companies simply follow a cost-plus approach to pricing their products or services. Many others have adopted market-based pricing. The few remaining companies have savvy managers who launch products at price points that reflect the value generated by their new product. U.S.

automobile manufacturers do sophisticated modeling for setting list prices using market surveys and various forms of conjoint (tradeoff) analysis. On the other hand, the same manufacturers lose control of prices after setting the sticker price, especially in the low-to-mid-priced category of cars.

Companies that have gained expertise through frequent new product launches operationalize the launch methodology with the help of "gated" processes to ensure quality throughout the launch process. There are predefined guidelines delineating the requirements and approval authorities for successful passage through a gate.

Consider the following company's example: A U.S.-based food products company has a gated process that starts with the business case that is supported by financial modeling with hypothetical prices and conducts product testing and taste tests among focus groups, and in many cases provides surveys to ascertain differentiation in taste with respect to their competition. Gatekeepers include multifunctional teams that ensure the project teams follow the product-launch process framework. When a process step does not meet the specification of the guidelines, the project team is sent back for rework until the requirements are met. At the final gate, the leadership team reviews a summary of the entire project due diligence process before providing support.

Despite this rigorous process involving scrubbing of internal data and seemingly in-depth competitive analysis, the senior executives at the food products company expressed frustration for not seeing meaningful results applied to the bottom line. The new product launches had failed to deliver the price gains they had expected from their investments. A review of the history of the last five important launches showed that the product teams did not have high confidence in their product mainly because the competitive data used was based on hearsay or often represented the worst-case scenario (bottom 5% pricing). As mentioned earlier, as a matter of practice, Sales would promise more sales, margins, and profits when asking for a new product. The product teams would pad the numbers to secure investment. As they successfully cleared different gates, their price forecast became increasingly conservative. At the time of launch or some time later, the realized price points reflected no growth or value differentiation between new and existing products.

The company improved the process significantly by including a pricing manager as an intermediate gatekeeper to help analyze the competitive price and related value analysis. The manager adapted the "cause-and-effect" matrix (refer to Chapter 7, "Tools for Six Sigma," for details on this tool), a Six Sigma tool as part of an exercise aimed at understanding the price and value. The resulting price-value map (Figure 5-2) provides a relative perception of value and average "street" price for the company vis-à-vis the competition.

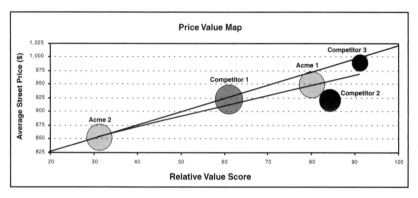

Figure 5-2 The price-value map shows relative price, relative value, and market share (size of bubble) of competing products

In this company, this process enhancement made it easier for the Product, Engineering, and Sales teams to agree on the value of their product relative to that of the competition based on ratings on a wide array of attributes based entirely on the knowledge residing within the company. Since implementing the process enhancement, price-point estimation moves from one gate to another only if the technical results prove different from those expected or if something changes in the competitive environment.

Product Lifecycle and Price

The price-value map shows a product in relation to competitors' products and applies to the company's other products as well. Thus, price is a portfolio issue in the sense that when a company introduces one product, it needs to consider the prices of the existing products that serve essentially the same customer needs.

Generally, as a product moves in its lifecycle, its price needs to be adjusted in relation to other products. Prices of older products may be relatively "higher" than new products because keeping inventory is costly especially if the demand has slowed over time, but prices may also be lower to emphasize the additional value of the newer products. Many companies try to lower inventory levels by seeking to manage demand using price, for example, by discounting low-selling items at a price break, running promotions to deplete slow burning product items, and so on and running prices up when trying to wean customers off products designated as obsolete.

With many manufacturing companies holding inventory in the thousands, sometimes hundreds of thousands of SKUs, there is a need to decrease manufacture-to-sell cycle time and to reduce inventory costs. The obvious solution—to manufacture and carry fewer line items—would be effective if it were easy to offer substitutes from within the product portfolio to customers buying these products.

As mentioned before, medical device companies thrive on innovation by launching newer generations of products constantly. One particular medical devices manufacturer maintains four to five products in their pacemaker portfolio, all of which fulfill the similar needs of regulating the rhythm of an ailing heart. These devices, implanted in the chest cavity just below the collarbone of a patient, differ in their value proposition based on the sophistication and effectiveness of correcting certain symptoms involving irregular heartbeat. The perceived value of these products depends on the weight and size because of the patient's comfort. It also depends on battery life that ranges from six to nine years because the patient would prefer to stay away from the surgeon's knife for a replacement as long as possible. Newer technology includes devices that are smaller and lighter and have greater battery life—to name a few enhancements.

Hence, the company expects price premium on newer products and constantly adjusts prices of existing product downwards in a one-to-two-year cycle. Given the high margins for medical devices (partly to adjust for high R&D costs), the key business objective is market share rather than realized price.

5.5 List Price Increase Due to Increase in Input Costs

Companies affected significantly from increases in the cost of raw materials or other inputs have to choose between increasing list prices and taking a hit to the bottom line. The increased price of gas, especially in 2005-2006, affected all transport-related industries—package delivery, airlines, consumer products, building materials, and even food products—as well as companies that use petroleum derivatives in manufacturing. Likewise, B2B manufacturers who are working with metals as raw material are finding themselves in world markets with tight supplies as China and India become increasingly industrialized. In such situations, companies launch price increases giving escalation in raw material costs as justification to their customers. When the time span of raw material cost inflation is uncertain and the customers are sensitive, some companies resort to levying surcharges to extract higher prices from customers while instilling confidence in their intent of keeping the increase only as long as the inflation lasts.

Many manufacturing companies have already cut costs through offshoring, outsourcing, downsizing, squeezing vendors, and switching to cheaper raw materials. Any more push in these directions could reduce their ability to compete effectively.

Companies are reticent about increasing list prices for a number of reasons:

- Regulators may suspect price fixing, especially if the companies in a particular industry have a history of rogue behavior.[1]
- Competitors react in unpredictable ways and may not follow the company's list price increase even when an entire industry faces lean times. They may view the price increase as an opportunity to increase volume.
- Customers may leave if the new list price is higher than similar competitive products. While transaction pricing can be customized to each transaction and therefore to the individual customer or customer-segment level, list price increases do not differentiate between customers located in different geographies or those having different purchasing guidelines.

- Implementing a list price increase and communicating it effectively to existing and new customers takes a great deal of effort. Managers may be unenthusiastic about meetings to build consensus as well as dealing with multiple IT systems and authorizations.

Still a company has to raise prices to increase profits. Compelling reasons for increasing list prices include inflation and increased industry demand, but a successful price increase requires customer acceptance and competitors' willingness to comply with a new "going rate." When there is inflation from rising costs of raw materials or due to change in industry regulations unmatched by gains in productivity, the immediate action by companies is to reduce expenditure, but after doing so, it has to rely on price increases to protect profits.

Case Study of Acme Raising List Price

This case study presents the circumstances at Acme to illustrate how it successfully implemented a list price increase. The point it proves is that price increases need to be thought through and implemented in a logical and diligent manner.

Acme anticipated demand growth after an extended lean period, but it was hit by large and unplanned cost inflation owing to steel and petroleum price hikes. The increase in steel costs alone meant millions of dollars of unplanned incremental costs on the horizon for Acme. They had already pared costs, and there was little more they could do to neutralize increased costs of steel and gasoline. Acme's suppliers refused to honor existing contracts and asked for higher prices.

Price increases seemed necessary, but Acme would have to implement these in a controlled manner to prevent loss of market share and profits. Too much of a price increase would mean losing revenue and profits, and too little would mean not being able to cover the increased costs.

Acme's major competitors—let's call them Zenith Corporation (35% market share) and Summit Inc. (18% market share)—were facing similar cost pressures due to the similarity of their product portfolios, location of manufacturing facilities, and extent of unionization in the labor force. Faced with sudden and sharp procurement cost increases, Acme had to choose among the following:

1. **Reduce the extent of discounting and promotions**: This, however, was something that the company had already been trying to do for some time, and its efforts had had only mixed results. Acme had realized some margin improvement, but pricing practices did not have much consistency or control. Further reduction in discounts could lead to loss in market share, which would be unacceptable in Acme culture.

2. **Use surcharges as a means to alleviate the cost burden**: Levying surcharges would be suitable and understood by customers if the inflationary force were temporary. However, the problem facing Acme seemed to be long term with China's growing steel consumption without expected matching increases in industry supply for several years.

3. **Increase list prices immediately**: This option would involve letting the customers and competitors know of the increase right away. This choice would provide the fastest relief if it could be implemented successfully. However, there were inherent risks in raising standard list prices due to the uncertainty in the market and lack of in-house experience with any similar action in recent years.

Acme implemented the list price increase in seven steps:

Step 1: **Determine how much price realization will fulfill business need**: The requirement for Acme to compensate for increased costs was to raise the price by at least 2%. However, it was important to aim slightly higher because the actual transaction prices (list price less discount) might not increase by the same proportion for all customers.

Step 2: **Understand price sensitivity of products relative to lifecycle or other factors**: Analysis of Acme's product line showed large variation in margins, sales, and maturity in the company's product offering. At one end was a mature product labeled as "commodity," owing to aggressive competitive pricing practices in recent years and its status as the biggest sales generator. According to Sales, customers would be quite sensitive to price increases for this product. At the other end there was a new product, just a year old, fulfilling specialized needs and enjoying relatively high prices but not growing as fast as planned. Acme could increase the price more easily for this product but had to be careful about slowing its sales growth further. Acme decided to frame the question regarding which products to increase the list price of relative to these two products.

Step 3: **Compare your products against those of competition**: Acme considered price-value maps (see Figure 5-2) based on feature-set comparisons to see how Acme products were perceived in the market vis-à-vis the competition. The "mature" product was pivotal in deciding the minimum list price increase. Its feature set offered more value than competitive products but had the same price or lower price than competitor products that offered the same "value." If Acme raised prices 2% (roughly the price differential with one competitor) and none of the competitors followed, it would be on par with this competitor at least and would be acting within reasonable bounds. However, if all competitors followed with a similar increase in list price, Acme's product would be better placed than before on the price-value map. The company did similar price value analyses with all major products. Therefore, a 2% increase at the mature product end (and a 3% increase at the new product end) was considered reasonable, although to realize such an increase in realized price, Acme would have to announce a list price increase more than this.

Step 4: **Predict and prepare for competitive reaction**: It was difficult to predict how the competition would react to a list increase, as there had been no such action in the industry in the past several years. The only clues available to predict competitive behavior were reactions at the time of new product launches. Acme had launched a high-end product a year prior with novel features and a price to skim the early adopter market. The main competitor had refrained from attacking this product with price as a weapon but had launched a similar product three months later. This allowed Acme to stay the course in its pricing strategy for its new product with this competitor's new product having a slightly lower price. The other competitor had tried to compete on price with its existing products but had found itself disadvantaged by the features of the new products offered by Acme and the other competitor. Acme felt it was more than likely that Zenith and others would follow their price leadership and pull up the pricing levels if they perceived Acme to be "serious" about price increases. Therefore, speed and clarity in announcing the price increase would be vital for Acme.

Step 5: Predict and prepare for customer reaction: Acme expected that customer reaction to the list price increase would vary by segment, transaction volume, and geographic location. Some customers might be more conscious of steel and petroleum price hikes and acquiesce in Acme's list price increase, while others who bought high-ticket items in large quantities would likely find the price increase undesirable. Acme decided to focus on its top 300 customers comprising of 65 to 70% sales volume and segmented them into three categories: *Economic*, *Value*, and *Loyal*. Acme management felt that some of the *Economic* customers would require persistent persuasion and continue to resist a price increase while *Value* and *Loyal* customers would be more accepting. While speed to act remained important, Acme was sensitive to its relationships with customers and wanted to provide a small but reasonable time window so that salespeople could clear outstanding commitments.

Step 6: Finalize plans and prepare Sales to execute list price increase: Acme decided to increase list prices by 3% on all products across-the-board and up to 5% on accessories. Using a 3% rather than a 2% increase would also help the company cover cost increases and establish clear price leadership to ensure that competition did not view this action as a guarded gesture but as true intent to raise prices. Conservative price-realization estimates showed that Acme would be able to overcome cost pressures and bring in incremental profit. In preparation, senior managers at Acme asked for analysis of sensitive national accounts, opportunity markets, and any large transactions in final stages of negotiation. A monthly review meeting was set up with representation from

Marketing, Sales, Finance, and Pricing to track the actual price realization and any hurdles in the process. The next step was to explain the price action to its Sales force before making an announcement in the press. The senior management forwarded a detailed memo to all the Sales managers outlining current cost pressures, urgency of implementation, and an action plan that included a timeline and selling message. Sales managers were instructed to start training the Sales personnel in how to initiate conversations with customers to prepare them for the price increases. Pricing and Marketing led phone and web meetings with major sales offices for training purposes and to hear objections in order to refine the message. In doing so, it became clear that there was general support throughout the organization.

Step 7: Communicate list increase to the market: Acme announced a list price increase in the main industry journal that brought to light latest innovations and significant news about industrial manufacturers and distributors. The announcement was made on July 5, with the effective date set at August 15 with an understanding that all pending customer negotiations would be cleared by September 15 of the same year.

RESULTS

Acme's competitors followed its lead. Zenith announced a 3% price increase on the very next day, and Summit followed suit a week later. The other smaller players in the industry seemed more cautious and took up to a month to announce smaller list-price increases. Zenith's announcement brought immediate relief, and managers at Acme were glad about having come through the exercise of affecting a list price increase unscathed. It soon became apparent that most of Acme's customers were expecting a price increase like they had seen from vendors from other industries. Senior management at Acme not only felt they solved the problem of margin erosion due to steel and petroleum price increases but that they could also get back to the original annual operating plan.

5.6 Promotions

Sales and Marketing personnel consider promotions to be an important tool in managing demand. A company typically uses promotions (1) to increase demand for a seasonal product or service in an off-peak season, (2) to induce customers to try newly launched products, (3) to decrease amount of product inventory, and (4) to grow sales quickly to meet the quarter's goal. Let us consider these contexts in turn.

Seasonal Pricing

Seasonal pricing is used not only by clothing retailers, hotels, and airlines but also by other industries. Clothing retailers tend to offer post-season discounts to entice the economic-minded yet value-seeking customer segment. The discounts make it easier to shake the perception of last season's fashion and helps burn inventory while a new fashion line-up still sells at higher average prices. Hotels and airlines charge peak season pricing during summer and Christmas holidays, while offering off-season or shoulder season pricing other times of the year. All seasonal industries use prices to manage demand. For instance, the hospitality industry plans for pricing in an annual cycle—peak, off-peak, and even shoulder-season pricing through revenue or yield management.

The airlines have gone a step further with day-of-week pricing and have structured ticket prices accordingly. Consider the example of a well-designed and executed promotion-related process at a large U.S.-based airline. The Executive Vice President of Marketing at this company would personally sign-off on every major promotion based on the analysis of baseline year sales, expected incremental revenue, expected dilution, cost of marketing materials, net incremental revenue, and finally return-on-investment (ROI). Prior to his sign-off, several individuals would follow a standardized process for putting the promotion into gear. The communication would flow from pricing analyst to pricing manager, pricing manager to marketing communication, marketing communication to legal, and finally to the VP within two or three days. The VP never failed to remind managers that he would be waiting for the post-analysis in a few months even though the analysis was already a part of the standard closed-loop process.

New Product Promotion

There are situations where customers eagerly await a company's products, for example, Sony's Play Station 3 just before Thanksgiving in 2006. However, not all new products share such good fortune. B2B manufacturers of specialized and highly technical products have to work harder at inducing trial by enticing customers with lower prices for some time.

These "lower prices" or promotions may be structured in different ways. In some industries like tooling, companies offer limited quantities of new product free of cost to targeted customers rather than risking customers feeling entitled to continuing low prices. By contrast, in the medical device companies, giving away free product is considered an illegal "inducement" in many countries. These and companies in many other industries run limited-time promotions to get attention for their products.

However, a promotion dilutes price and profit and assumes the demand will be low, an assumption that may be incorrect. Moreover, if a promotion is successful in increasing demand for the product, the increase in unit sales may mean a long-term hit to the company's profitability.

In the case of a particular B2B manufacturer, the promotion for a new product generated so much demand that the unit sales wiped out months of projected profits and detracted from the product's deserved high-value/high-price position. Such a failure can be due to poor planning in estimating demand or due to poor execution in bringing realized prices back up from the "limited-time" promotion.

Inventory Reduction Promotions

Price promotions to reduce inventory are a common sight in many industries especially where manufacture-to-sell cycle time is monitored closely by analysts. Industrial manufacturers also try to extract additional sales at the end of a quarter or year as "inventory-reduction" sales even though the purpose is to meet or exceed goals.

The downside is that customers get used to this situation and hold off from purchasing until a large discount is available at the end of the quarter or year. Pricing managers in many companies complain about quarter-end deals, but these companies and their customers have locked themselves into a situation that repeats every quarter, every year. These companies have to build large inventories to plan for end-of-quarter (or month or year) sales. The "inventory reduction" sale, therefore, effectively increases the inventory! This is why many products in many retail stores have every-day low prices rather than promotions.

Vendor-managed inventory (VMI) is inventory that is maintained at the customer's location but still shows up on the company's books. The customer is invoiced when they use the product. Ordinarily, the price of this product should be higher than in other situations because keeping the inventory on the customer's site is an additional service to the customer. However, when contract terms are weak to begin with or the company does not or cannot insist on adherence to contract terms, the customer may demand lower prices for reducing inventory.

5.7 Discount-setting and Concession Process

Setting the discounts or giving concessions in individual transactions is a process prone to price and profit leaks. Yet senior management in any company typically does not intervene unless things get out of hand. Acme's case study in Chapter 3, "Case Study—Pricing Operations and Six Sigma Pricing," illustrates some of the many possible problems that B2B and even B2C companies face with respect to the discounting process.

Discounts typically apply to individual transactions or spot sales, however, even where there are contracts and contract pricing in place. Individual transactions may be occasionally "sweetened" in the hope for additional sales. Another variation on discounts is to relax the contract terms, for instance by charging the prices as those specified in the contract even when the volume purchased by the customer is much lower than that anticipated in the contract.

5.8 Analysis, Report, and Review Processes

For senior management to better control prices, it is essential that they monitor pricing processes. The link that closes the loop on processes is measurement and tracking. As illustrated by the example of promotions at a U.S.-based airline whose executive VP personally monitored the post-analysis of every promotion, companies in low-margin industries excel at tracking the results of their pricing actions. However, in general, B2B companies lag in this area and suffer the consequences of deferring to "gut feel" while missing the rich information about customers and market opportunities stored within their transactional databases.

Generating reports is easy given the use of computers and databases in companies, but their use in tracking results and in planning is another matter. Consider the example of a $5 billion division of a major industrial manufacturer that had a user-friendly web-based reporting tool. A Sarbanes-Oxley-related project required a closer check on the reports generated and displayed on this tool. The company found a staggering number of active reports related to pricing—over 200 of these issued by people or automatically on a daily, monthly, or quarterly basis. Among these, the reports with a common theme sometimes did not have matching numbers. Moreover, fewer than 20 were in use by anyone in a position to make a business decision.

Two things are of utmost importance for improving pricing operations in any company: first, analytical capability that converts data into information and second, leadership interest in reviewing the qualitative and quantitative information together. Many large airlines follow a focused revenue-and-yield (price per mile) review process.

Pricing processes to track compliance may include measuring and tracking success of pricing initiatives; tracking prices for consigned or vendor-managed inventory; and comparing actual transaction prices and volumes against those specified in the contract.

5.9 Summary

There are two categories of pricing processes at the operational level to implement pricing strategy. These are: (1) processes to ensure that the list prices remain "current" by means of changes in response to changes in the market environment and (2) processes to ensure adherence to pricing guidelines. The latter seek to achieve high levels of price realization (relative to list prices). As an example, designing a price promotion for *new* customers is a (temporary) price change, but we also need processes to ensure that the promotion is carried out as designed. For instance, the price changes apply only to new customers and not to existing ones; otherwise, dollar sales may actually fall because of the "promotion."

The first category includes the situation in which a company with lots of new products throughout the year will have new product launch pricing as part of pricing operations rather than strategy. Modifying the price of a product throughout its lifecycle, especially as new and improved products displace it from the market gradually, is another process. Even where list prices are set once in a year or once every few years, processes are needed to change list prices much more frequently because of jumps in the prices of commodities or energy. Temporary changes in list prices due to seasonal pricing or price promotions also need well-defined processes. A pricing strategy may be in place, but companies need processes to fine-tune the strategy and list prices (or pricing guidelines) for different channels, for global customers, for intermediaries, for end customers, and for contracts.

The second category includes analyze-report-and-review processes. For instance, there may be a monthly meeting reviewing the average price change (relative to previous month) by region, product line, channel, and so on and the resulting increase or decrease in revenue. Companies can monitor contract compliance using existing systems. Reporting on such compliance should occur regularly, and care needs to be taken that these reports support and inform planning and decision making.

—

6
SIX SIGMA

Statistical thinking will one day be as necessary for
efficient citizenship as the ability to read and write.

—*H. G. Wells*

6.1 Introduction

There are many books on Six Sigma, but there remains much confusion about the topic, part of which is about whether Six Sigma is an application of statistics and whether it is only a fad or a philosophy—or even a revelation. Our view is that Six Sigma is a tool, a very useful one, but only a tool nonetheless. As a tool, Six Sigma is useful in the hands of those who know what they want and what to do with it and useless or even dangerous in the hands of others.

Six Sigma methodology aims for eliminating defects in any repeated manufacturing, service, or other process, using a disciplined, data-driven approach. The statistical representation of the defect level of a process in Six Sigma terms describes how it is performing vis-à-vis customer expectations or other specifications. The "defect" is in the eye of the customer, or at least as perceived by the provider.

6.2 Historical Background

Predecessors of Six Sigma are Statistical Process Control (SPC) and Total Quality Management (TQM) among others.[1]

Statistical Process Control

SPC, also known as SQC, came into being through the initial use of statistics for industrial purposes by Walter A. Shewhart, who implemented the use of control charts in the communications industry in 1924. He advocated the use of statistics for quality control of manufacturing processes.

The focus of SPC is on monitoring processes to minimize variation in the process and consequently in the output by imposing controls. The basic steps include measuring and tracking the outcome of a process to identify when the process goes "out of control" due to a problem. This problem can then be identified and corrected to eliminate the variance in the process so that it gives consistent output.

Shewhart's pupil, W. Edwards Deming, continued his work and developed a theory of management based on the foundational principles that Shewhart had developed for manufacturing processes. Deming did not have much success convincing American businesses, in particular the auto industry, to adopt his methods. However, Japanese manufacturers, who were in the progress of rebuilding their economy after World War II, realized significant gains through implementing Deming's principles and consequently made inroads into the U.S. market, especially in the auto market.

Of all the Japanese auto manufacturers, Toyota is the one most associated with quality and quality management. It has developed the Toyota Production System that motivated Lean Manufacturing, a philosophy similar to but not the same as Six Sigma.

Total Quality Management (TQM)

Although the principles of TQM are synonymous with Japanese management, the coining of the term and widespread adoption of TQM began in the United States. This was at a time when the United States was facing arguably one of the major management issues of the last 20 years, that of the poor quality of American products and services, and consequently its decrease in competitiveness in global markets.

American consumers began to move to higher quality foreign imports. This was quite visible in the automobile industry where Japanese manufacturers began to gain market share at the expense of domestic manufacturers in the U.S. market. Under threat, big U.S. industrial giants followed suit, popularizing the concept in the mainstream as a result.

Unlike SPC that focuses on individual processes, TQM seeks to improve customer satisfaction through an integrated effort from all areas of a business, toward continuous improvement of the quality of services. Note that the principles of the TQM school of thought emphasize customer satisfaction for services, even though its initial application was predominantly in the manufacturing sector.

The end-to-end approach works on a systems basis, preaching that the output from a cohesive effort is greater than the sum of its parts. A strategy based on TQM focuses on customer satisfaction by targeting improvement at all levels and encouraging employee involvement at all stages. A key assumption in this philosophy is that of continuous improvement. In other words, there is always room for improvement, thus allowing defects to be eventually reduced to zero. Such thinking forms the basis for Six Sigma and other quality initiatives.

Six Sigma

A Motorola engineer by the name of Bill Smith developed the tools and mathematics for Six Sigma and is credited for the term in reference to the method of approaching business problems with a statistical toolset. He referred to Six Sigma as "organized common sense." Another person from Motorola, Mikel Harry, constructed a methodology around the concept with his paper, "The Strategic Vision for Accelerating Six Sigma Within Motorola."

Six Sigma was first launched in 1987 at Motorola, which had been suffering from customer dissatisfaction, high operating costs, shrinking market share, and increasing warranty costs.[2] The CEO, Bob Galvin, and other executives traveled to sites worldwide to explain this initiative. The Six Sigma that exists today is a combination of both a data-driven and change-management methodology, created and promoted by Mikel Harry and Richard Schroeder, another ex-Motorola executive.

The next company to pick up Six Sigma was the conglomerate Allied Signal. General Electric's CEO Jack Welch was impressed with the turn-around at Allied Signal and invited their CEO to present at GE University, which is how Six Sigma arrived at GE.

Six Sigma was particularly suited to the manufacturing environment due to its aim of controlling variation in the output quality and that this arena tends to be well equipped for data driven initiatives with the most process metrics already having been developed. Jack Welch is said to have remarked that Six Sigma's ability to control variation of a reasonable quality product was more valued by customers than a higher quality product on average but with greater variation in quality. Through adoption of this disciplined approach, it is possible to improve productivity and eliminate waste. GE has claimed the approach resulted in approximately $10 billion savings in the first five years of running Six Sigma projects.

6.3 Why Six Sigma and Not Five or Seven

Let us first explain the literal meaning of Six Sigma and then discuss that this is really only a metaphor for our context, that is, Pricing. The phrase "Six Sigma" literally implies a goal of reducing the number of defects to less than 3.4 defects per million occurrences, assuming that the quality of the selected measure has a normal bell-shaped distribution pattern across millions of measurements. The first question is why 3.4 and not 5.4 or 1.6? There is no particular reason other than the fact that for the normal distribution—the particular bell-shaped distribution that explains the relative proportion of quality attributes of manufactured items—has exactly 3.4 "defects" out of a million if the acceptable limits are set at three standard deviations from the mean on either side (see Figure 6-1). It is from these six standard deviations that Six Sigma gets its name—the Greek letter sigma denotes standard deviation.

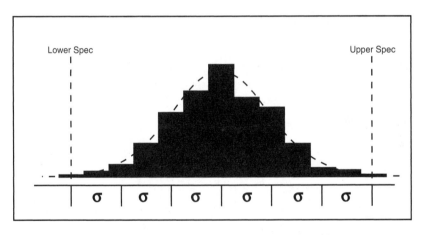

Figure 6-1 The bell-shaped normal distribution showing the proportion
of defects or items outside the acceptable limits

To achieve Six Sigma level of quality, a process must not produce more than 3.4 defects per million opportunities literally—when the number of defects is higher, the Sigma level is correspondingly lower (see Table 6-1). In statistical parlance, the Sigma level is the number of standard deviations of occurrences within specifications.

For a given set of specifications around the mean, if the standard deviation is small, that is, the process has little variance, the greater the number of standard deviations fit within these specifications and therefore more percentage process outcomes meet these specifications. Conversely, if the process runs poorly, it will produce widely varying results with high standard deviation around the mean. Therefore, fewer standard deviations can fit within the specifications. In other words, fewer percentage outcomes meet these specifications and there are more percentage defects.

Just as a process with a defect rate of less than 0.00034% is at 6-sigma performance level, a process for which the defect rate is about 31% sits at 2-sigma level. A 0.6% defect rate qualifies a process at 4-sigma level.

Table 6-1 Defects When Specifications Around the Mean Are at a Given Sigma Level

Sigma Level	Defects per Million	% Defective	% Nondefective
2	308,537	30.85%	69.1%
3	66,807	6.68%	93.32%
4	6,210	0.62%	99.379%
5	233	0.023%	99.9767%
6	3.4	0.00034%	99.99966%

There are two issues when we talk about Six Sigma Pricing in realistic rather than conceptual settings. First, in pricing you should not be surprised if you find processes at less than 2-sigma level of performance, that is, with a defect rate of more than a third. Moving to Six Sigma in any realistic time frame may be impossible. Therefore, moving even to a 4-sigma level or 5% defect rate, let alone 6-sigma level, may be quite a challenge.

Six Sigma and Pricing

However, Six Sigma does not have to taken literally to mean lowering process variation and hence standard deviation so much that the acceptable limits exceed six standard deviations, and the defect rate falls to less than 3.4 out of a million occurrences. There are at least three reasons:

- First, a project, Six Sigma or otherwise, is not a failure if it reduces the defect rate from 20% to 3% simply because it did not get below the magic number of 3.4 parts in a million! In a pricing project, it is unlikely you will get anywhere close to 3.4 excessive *discounts* per million transactions when an excessive discount is defined as a defect. However, improving the defect rate from 20% to 15% could add millions of dollars to annual profits and it is therefore worth achieving.
- Second, these conversions of defect rates into Sigma levels assumes that the attribute being measured for quality has a bell-shaped or "normal" curve denoting the probability distribution of the attribute being measured that determines whether or not the widget or the price is a "defect." This may not always be the case—for pricing projects, the distribution of prices (or discounts) across thousands of transactions is skewed and could be thought of as being "lognormal" rather than being "normal."
- Finally, another assumption is that defects lie on both tails, but in many pricing projects, you may be interested only in one side, for example, realized price being too low (worry less about the realized price being too high unless this happens often). Turnaround time for price approvals in the company being too long may be a defect, but no customer or salesperson would complain if the turnaround times were "too short."

Indeed, in many nonmanufacturing situations, the distribution of the output measure will generally not be bell-shaped or "normal."[3] For instance, operational loss amounts per loss event for banks tend to have highly skewed distributions like lognormal or gamma rather than the symmetrical normal distribution. The time taken by pricing analysts to respond to salespersons' requests for price approval or the time taken to service IT requests in a company also has a skewed distribution. In these situations, we cannot talk about six standard deviations as if the distribution is normal or expect the Sigma calculation to have any meaning.

However, in all cases whether or not related to pricing, we can use Six Sigma as a metaphor to reduce standard deviations, that is, the variations in repeatable processes so that (almost) all occurrences are within acceptable limits.

6.4 Misperceptions of Six Sigma

Given the history of previous quality movements that have come and gone in many companies, there is fear in some of these companies that Six Sigma would simply add to bureaucracy. It can certainly do that if applied mindlessly as a requirement to all promotion and all investment decisions. As mentioned before, companies need to view it as a useful tool but simply a tool all the same. Deployed properly, it should decrease rather than increase bureaucracy.

Six Sigma is one more quality approach on the heels of SPC and TQM, along with other approaches such as Quality Improvement (QI) Storyboard and Lean Manufacturing, the latter based on the famed Toyota Production System. There are important differences just as there are important elements shared by all these approaches. Which one should a company use?

Consider an analogy of kitchen knives. A good chef will know when to use which one and to what effect. The chef will also know that in some cases the choice does not matter at all which one to use. However, even people comfortable with the different quality approaches may not fully appreciate their differences and similarities or their applicability to particular situations. As such, in a company situation the choice of quality approach boils down to faith, that is, making Six Sigma or Lean Manufacturing appear closer to religious dogma than to a systematic rational data-and-fact based approach. The result can be holy wars if there are competing adherents to different approaches. However, just as a good chef uses different knives depending on the need, a company should be open to using different approaches as applicable.

Even in companies where Six Sigma has won recognition as providing genuine value based on these companies' own experiences, non-manufacturing groups damn Six Sigma with faint praise as being a good "manufacturing" tool. In other words, these groups would prefer

Six Sigma to stay in the factory. When we bring up the idea that the goal is to improve processes whether they are in the factory or in the tenth floor of corporate headquarters, we sometimes elicit the response that there is no process—and that none is needed. Ironically, such a response usually indicates serious problems regarding poorly defined or understood processes, thereby highlighting the need for Six Sigma.

Yet another source of confusion about Six Sigma pertains to the literal, and all too liberal, use of the phrase "up to 3.4 defects per million" or 0.00034%. People in Pricing or Finance or other nonmanufacturing groups may not grasp "millions of instances." For instance, if a defect is noncompliance to service level agreements in an IT support environment, it is difficult to envision "millions" of service calls. A defect rate of 3.4 per million seems (and is) unbelievable in such an environment where more than 50% of the service calls may be noncompliant! Think of Six Sigma as continuous improvement whereby the defect rate is reduced from 55% to 45% and then to 35% rather than to 0.00034%.

There is also confusion about benefits of Six Sigma. We should separate out two types of benefits pertaining respectively to Six Sigma as a journey and to the outcome of a completed Six Sigma project resulting in a reduced defect rate. The benefits of building a culture where defects are not tolerated and where all processes are run tightly result from Six Sigma as a journey. The dollar savings that result are the benefits of completed Six Sigma projects.

6.5 Application of Six Sigma to Non-manufacturing Situations

In many non-manufacturing situations, an often-occurring challenge is that the high variability in the time to do something is variable. Consider IT support in a company. If IT support is outsourced to another company, and sometimes even if it is within the company, there may be a service level agreement (SLA) in place that says that 80% of all calls must be resolved within four hours, 90% within 24 hours, and 99% within four days. In reality perhaps only half the calls are resolved within four hours, and only 70% within 24 hours. Even after four days, more than 10% of the calls may be unresolved.

If we were to make a frequency plot of the times of all resolved calls, we would not get a symmetric bell-shaped curve resembling a normal distribution. The distribution would be skewed—think of bell curve squished on one side—with a limit of zero hours on one side and a diminishingly small number of calls stretching on to the right with long times.

If the IT support group of the company were to improve its processes such that the variation in response time reduced, the proportion of calls resolved within the SLA-specific limits would decrease. Of course, a "creative" way to lower the defect rate is to log related tasks as separate calls to increase the proportion of calls that can be handled quickly, but this is not a result of process improvement or Six Sigma.

There are other time-based defects. Consider number of days outstanding on accounts receivable from customers. Despite the terms stated in a sales transaction—2% discount for cash, all amount due within 30 days, some accounts receivable may stretch to a few months, and in our experience, even to more than two years in one case.

6.6 Five Steps of a Six Sigma Project (DMAIC)

The fundamental objective of the Six Sigma methodology is the implementation of a measurement-based process improvement through variation reduction. This is accomplished through Six Sigma sub-methodologies for process improvement—this is "DMAIC" and is the one of interest to us—and for design and new product development. Once a senior person in a company, along with other senior colleagues, has selected a project and elected a project sponsor and a team or at least a team lead, we can get into the Six Sigma steps.

DMAIC, pronounced (Duh-May-Ick), is an acronym for five interconnected steps of a process improvement project: Define, Measure, Analyze, Improve, and Control. Thankfully, there are only five phases and not six because otherwise some people would assume that six in Six Sigma refers to the number of phases. We mention this only because it has come up in discussions with those new to Six Sigma. The objective is to improve existing processes falling below specification and look for incremental improvement. The approach is data-driven, and each step in the cyclical DMAIC process is required to ensure the best possible results.[4]

1. **Define:** The first step in any Six Sigma project is to clarify the problem and narrow its scope in such a way that the project team can achieve measurable goals within a few months. Then a team is assembled to examine the process in detail, to suggest improvements, and to implement those recommendations. With manufacturing projects, project managers and their sponsors typically begin by defining what constitutes a defect and then establishing a set of objectives designed to reduce the occurrence of such defects. *Define* can include the following:

   - Define the customer, their Critical to Quality (CTQ) issues, and the Core Business Process involved
   - Define who customers are, what their requirements are for products and services, and what their expectations ar.
   - Define project boundaries—the stop and start of the process
   - Define the process to be improved by mapping the process flow

2. **Measure:** In the second step of a Six Sigma project, the team maps the process, gathers data, verifies the quality of data, and prepares it for analysis:

   - Measure the performance of the Core Business Process involved
   - Develop a data collection plan for the process
   - Collect data from many sources to determine types of defects and metrics
   - Compare to customer survey results to determine shortfall

3. **Analyze:** Once a process has been mapped and documented, and the quality of the hard data supporting it has been verified, the Six Sigma team can begin the analysis. The team members usually start by meeting to identify the ways in which people fail to act as needed or fail to assert effective control at each stage:

   - Analyze the data collected and process map to determine root causes of defects and opportunities for improvement

- Identify gaps between current performance and goal performance
- Prioritize opportunities to improve and,
- Identify sources of variation

4. **Improve**: The team identifies improvements based on the analysis undertaken. In other words, the suggested improvements must be backed by hard data and analysis:

   - Improve the target process by designing creative solutions to fix and prevent problems
   - Create innovative solutions using technology and discipline
   - Develop and deploy implementation plan

5. **Control**: In the final stage of a Six Sigma project, the team creates controls that enable the company to sustain and extend the improvements:

   - Control the improvements to keep the process on the new course
   - Prevent reverting back to the "old way"
   - Require the development, documentation, and implementation of an ongoing monitoring plan
   - Institutionalize the improvements through the modification of systems and structures (staffing, training, incentives)

6.7 Summary

Six Sigma has been around formally since the late 1980s when a Motorola engineer coined the term for quantifying process variability and defects. Since then, not just Motorola, but also other companies like Allied Signal and GE have benefited greatly from widespread use of Six Sigma in their manufacturing and service processes. However, the principles behind Six Sigma have been around since at least the 1920s in the work of Shewhart. The same principles of statistics and quality control show up in Total Quality Management (TQM) and Statistical Process Control (SPC). As such, Six Sigma is not a fad and even if it does go out of fashion, the principles will survive.

There are a few misperceptions of Six Sigma. One is around the term itself and taking it too literally to mean at most 3.4 defects per million. A second is that it requires advanced statistics—it requires rigor in data analysis, but using statistics does not ensure rigor, and rigor may not require advanced statistics. A third is that it applies only to manufacturing. In reality, it applies to any repeated process where one can measure the output unambiguously to classify the output as being defective or not. Finally, while the goal of any Six Sigma effort is to reduce the defect rate to lower than 3.4 per million, this is not the goal of any one Six Sigma project. Instead, Six Sigma is a continuous improvement approach that you can use to reduce the defect rate incrementally through successive projects. The same applies to pricing as well.

There are five stages of any Six Sigma project:

1. The first is to define, i.e., to quantify the problem and state the goal.

2. The second is to measure, i.e., to detail the as-is process and collect different types of data for analysis in the next stage.

3. The third is to analyze the process and the data to determine the causes of variation.

4. The fourth is for the project team to make recommendations to improve the process.

5. The final stage is for the team to recommend various controls on the process as part of the control phase to lower the process variation and to ensure that the improvements are actually taking place.

7
TOOLS FOR SIX SIGMA

We shall not fail or falter…Give us the tools
and we will finish the job.

—*Sir Winston Churchill (1874–1965)*

7.1 Introduction

There are many tools for Six Sigma Pricing, and these are no different from those for other Six Sigma projects. We emphasize that these tools are exactly that: tools. We may use these or ignore these as we see fit and modify them or discard them midway through a project based on our need. They are not artifacts of some ritual, and we should not feel we have to use each of them or in any particular sequence except where it makes sense in a particular project or context.

However, there is a difference between use of tools in pricing projects and in nonpricing projects, at least in degree. The emphasis on using tools for Six Sigma Pricing should be on simplicity and on clear communication rather than on sophistication. While this should be true in general, this is especially important for Six Sigma Pricing because of the multiple functions and groups involved in any Six Sigma Pricing project with their divergent interests and incentives.

There is no shortage of tools, ranging from the simplest to the most sophisticated. Moreover, for a given tool, there are many variants in use by different proponents and by different users. Our aim for this chapter is not to provide an encyclopedia but an orientation as to what tools can be useful and when. There are a few excellent books with templates and tips that get into tools in greater detail than this chapter does, such as titles by Thomas Pyzdek[1] and Forrest Breyfogle III.[2] George Eckes[3] provides 10 technical tools and 10 "soft" tools, as well.

7.2 Tools for the Define Phase

The Define phase can be a mini-project in itself, so tools used in other phases of a Six Sigma project are useful here and vice versa. However, in most projects, we use simple tools to quantify and convey the extent of the "problem" at hand.

Critical-to-Quality Tree

This is data collection in the form of a tree of needs for the customer—in case of pricing, the multiple stakeholders. Again, this is a group effort, so the purpose is to share knowledge and build a shared understanding. We start with the customer's (stakeholder's) view and identify needs one by one. Then we break this need into subneeds and then into things that can actually be measured. The measures are critical to achieve quality and a desirable outcome (see Figure 7-1).

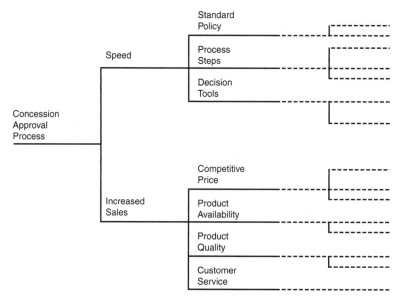

Figure 7-1   Example of a Critical-to-Quality Tree

High-level Process Map

We can identify a process, as is currently followed, showing inputs and outputs at each substep. As with any process description, we can do this at any level. The high-level process is the entire process seen as a single step, and a more detailed one will have a few subprocesses, each with inputs being the outputs of the preceding subprocesses. At the Define phase, we can use a high-level process map to show we have understood the process.

A process map describes the process visually. For purposes of the Define phase, we could stick to the process as more-or-less than it should be. For pricing processes, we will find that there is a gap, sometimes a big one, between what the process is and what it should be (see Figure 7-2).

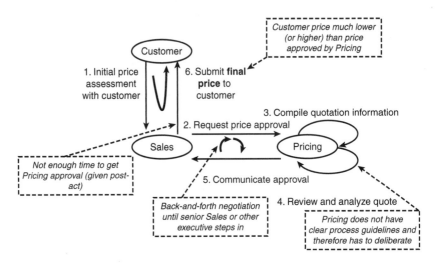

Figure 7-2   Example of a high-level process map

Stakeholder Analysis

One thing that could be useful for Six Sigma Pricing projects is to list stakeholders and score them on a scale of 1 to 5 on two dimensions: (1) on their power (title, clout, and so on) and (2) on their interest in making the project successful—with 1 for "resistant or low," 3 for "neutral," and 5 for "supportive or high." The project advocate should then score the extent to which their assistance will be needed during the project and its eventual implementation, again between a scale of 1 to 5—1 for "not needed at all" and 5 for "needed very much." The entire stakeholder set can be framed as in Figure 7-3.

- **High power, interested people**: These are the people we must fully engage and make the greatest efforts to satisfy.
- **High power, less interested people**: Put enough work in with these people to keep them satisfied but not so much that they become bored with the message.
- **Low power, interested people**: Keep these people adequately informed and talk to them to ensure that no major issues are arising. These people can often be very helpful with the details of the project.
- **Low power, less interested people**: Monitor these people.

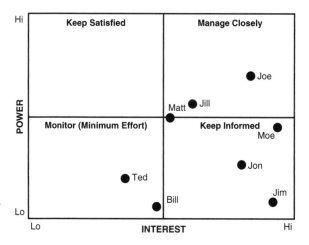

Figure 7-3   Example of stakeholder analysis

The team leader needs to understand the individuals' reasons for resistance, especially from people with power and influence, and figure out how to win them over.[4] This step may be critical in B2B environments where different functional groups have different views on the role of pricing.

This analysis is not for presentation. Instead, a project advocate should use this analysis to get help in getting critical people involved in the break down of potential barriers. Stakeholder analysis is a useful tool for pricing professionals to manage their sources of support as well as resistance.

Descriptive Statistics for a Single Quantity

Averages, percentiles, ranges, standard deviation, and many other statistics describe only one attribute of whatever we are measuring. These statistics are termed "univariate" because they describe only one variable by itself. For instance, the attribute of interest may be the discount over all completed transactions for a particular family of products. Using the last three months' transactions as a sample, we can obtain the discount for each transaction and then present the discount as a statistic in a variety of ways—average, median, mode for the "typical" discount and range, standard deviation, tenth and ninetieth percentiles, and so on for the variability of the discount for transactions around this "typical" value. Pie charts, bar charts, frequency diagrams, and histograms are different ways of graphically presenting the same information.

We should emphasize two points. The first is about how the sample is taken to obtain the numbers. If the data are highly seasonal, it is not correct to use the last three months as a sample because then the numbers would depend on where in the year the last three months fall. In this case we may be better off getting a random sample of transactions from one or two years of data.

The second is about which particular measure is better to use in the context. Again, this depends on the nature of the data. For instance, house prices in London vary over a huge range. If we were to make a frequency diagram, we would get a long-tailed distribution with a few houses and flats that are priced in the tens of millions of pounds and several houses and flats in the below £300,000 category. Here we use the median, or the fiftieth percentile, the transaction price above and below which are half of the houses on the market. The reason is that the median is less susceptible to changes in the extreme values and is therefore more amenable to tracking. Likewise, in pricing, many more transactions will have discounts closer to zero than to 100%, so the distribution is skewed. Using different percentiles—the median is the fiftieth percentile but we can also use the tenth and ninetieth percentiles as well, which may give a better sense of the "typical" discount than the average discount.

Commonly used graphics to describe the "problem" and its severity are pie charts and bar charts. We use pie charts to express proportions or percentages and bar charts to express numbers of different types. We can also use bar charts to display trends such as increasing number of incidents per month for several months in a row.

Consider the following example: A business group has outsourced its IT needs to a vendor, and there is a service-level agreement in place that says that 95% or more of the calls should be satisfactorily handled (from the user's viewpoint) within 24 hours of first making the call and the remainder within four days. In reality, the vendor is able to handle only 55% of the calls satisfactorily within the first 24 hours and 80%

within four days. We could then simply describe the problem with a pie chart that shows 55% of calls being "OK," another 25% being "late," and the remaining 20% being "excessively late." Thus we can use a pie chart that describes the status of all completed tasks: "OK," "late," and "excessively late" (see Figure 7-4).

IT Requests by Status

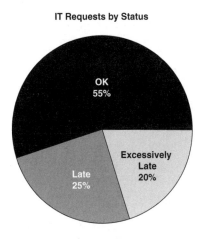

Figure 7-4   Example of a pie chart

However, there is a better way to describe the problem at hand. We could summarize the time to complete all requests. We could do this using a frequency chart showing what percentage of calls take what number of hours or days. More appropriately, we could use a histogram (see Figure 7-6), the difference being that the attribute in a histogram is a continuous variable like time (for example, 24.5 hours) rather than a category (like the type of status). Instead of using the status type of jobs for a sample of 100 calls, we use the difference in time stamps to describe the time taken.

When we have categories such as "low," "medium," and "high" for the attribute in question, we can use a frequency diagram.

When these categories are for continuous data, for instance with discount levels across all transactions, then a histogram is used instead of a frequency diagram (8–10 hours, 10–15 hours, 15–20 hours, and so on). The only visual difference between the two is that frequency diagrams have gaps between the bars whereas histograms have none to reflect that the data on the X-axis are continuous (see Figure 7-5).

For instance, if we had many transactions each with its own discount level ranging from, say 30% to 70%, we can make a histogram with bins ranging from 30 to 40, 40 to 50, 50 to 60, 60 to 70 and so on. Spreadsheet packages such as Microsoft Excel provide add-on tools to make histograms.

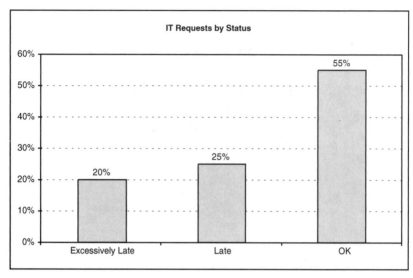

Figure 7-5   Example of a frequency diagram

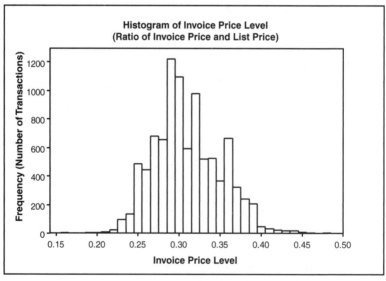

Figure 7-6   Example of a histogram

Paretos charts are named after the Italian economist Pareto who is also associated with the popularly quoted, but often misunderstood, 80–20 rule. He is also associated with the "long tail." The diagram is an ordered frequency diagram or histogram where the highest frequency bin comes first, and the lowest frequency bin comes last. Such a diagram is quite useful to visually show the most frequent types of defects or causes of defects.

A Pareto chart (see Figure 7-7) can help with scoping even when it presents the same information as a pie chart (see Figure 7-4) or a frequency chart (see Figure 7-5). If for instance, we use the Pareto diagram to find that the percentage discount is higher for one region than others, we could do a project on this region alone initially. A Pareto chart helps with scoping because it conveys quickly how the regions are ordered in terms of decreasing number of defectively priced transactions.

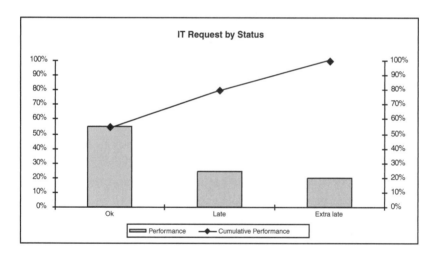

Figure 7-7   Example of a Pareto diagram

7.3 Tools for the Measure Phase

In the Measure phase, any Six Sigma project focuses on measuring different aspects of a process to set the phase for analysis in the following phase. We need tools for describing the process in its current state as well as tools for figuring out which data to collect and how. We use

SIPOC (see the following section) for describing the process and design of experiments (DOE) for setting up the data. In addition, some process analysis can take place in the Measure phase, but we describe all analysis-related tools in the next section.

SIPOC

SIPOC stands for *supplier-inputs-process-outputs-customer* and is a chart or a table identifying the inputs and outputs of the process in question, along with the suppliers of the inputs and the consumers of the outputs (see Figure 7-8). As with any process description, we can do this at any level, but the detail should be enough to allow examination of how the output of the process or any subprocess is connected with which inputs and of how the actual process differs from that intended. Indeed, for pricing processes, we will find that there is a gap, sometimes a big one, between what the process is and what it should be. However, this is the sort of detailed process mapping that we will be doing in the Measure phase following the high-level map in the Define phase.

Design of Experiments (DOE)

Statistical DOE is a structured approach used to find out how the output measure of interest, for example, percent discount, varies with various inputs called *main effects*—for instance, sales region and transaction size—and their combinations called *interaction effects*. Such a design is carried out before the "experiment" or process that would generate the input data that would produce varying output data. For pricing, the data will already have been created by way of various contracts or list prices or discounts off the list prices in actual transactions. Still, it is useful to go through a DOE exercise to structure the data collection—decide on which bits of data to compile—and check whether these would answer the questions being sought on root-causes or controls.

Step	Supplier	Controlled (C) Uncontrolled (U)	Input	Process	Output	Customer
1	Sales rep. Sales Manager	(U)	Name price sensitive	Identify Key Accounts and sales growth	Shortlist customers	Pricing, Sales Management, Senior
2	Who supplies data or information in this step? How – by phone, fax, or in-person, etc.	Is this step in control–Is it working or can it be made to work with relative ease	What is the information supplied in the process step?	What happens in this step?	What is the information outflow or result of the process step?	Who is the recipient of the output in this step?
3						
4			potential sales.	approve price, validate	step 3	
5	Customer	(U)	Final Proposal	Reviews proposal and signs if agreement; If no agreement, go back to	Signed contract	Sales Rep, Pricing
6	Pricing	(C)	Updates order entry system with pricing details	Line item update in order entry system	New customer pricing updated	Sales, Customer
7	Pricing	(C)	Annual sales and margin data	Annual audit of sales activity vs. expectation	Action plan to grow or maintain account	Sales and Senior management

Figure 7-8   SIPOC example

Typically, once we have an output measure, we need to decide on which inputs (X's) we will focus to identify main and interaction effects. Using the example of Acme, if the discount level in invoice data is the output measure of interest, our inputs may be total invoice amount, sales region of delivery, time of year, type of customer, and so on. Some of these may be discrete ("chunky" or categories like sales region or product line) and others continuous (varying smoothly like transaction amount).

The possible settings of the input factors are called levels, and any distinct combination of input factors and levels is called a treatment. For instance, any line item in an invoice is a treatment because it has the output, that is, percentage discount off list price, as well as the sales region, total invoice amount, and so on. We need to have many replications of any treatment to produce output data—in our example, many invoices. There are many ways to produce different replications for different treatments, and we refer to books on statistics or to technical books on Six Sigma.[5]

DOE is useful for Six Sigma Pricing projects in the Measure phase because it helps us figure out the relationships we are trying to establish, for example, answering questions such as whether some regions give higher discounts than others, and if they do, is it because they have customers who generate large invoices. However, the data we will likely be using in such projects will already be in place, and we would not actually be running "experiments." What data to collect using the "data collection plan" is discussed later in Chapter 10, "Measure Phase."

In addition we have to consider whether the data we have collected (or will collect) accurately measures what we intended to measure using something called Measurement Systems Analysis (MSA) discussed in Chapter 10.

7.4 Tools for the Analyze Phase

There are three types of analyses pertaining to the process we want to improve: (1) *process analysis* to identify process failures that lead to a defective output, (2) *root-cause analysis* to hypothesize reasons for defects and validating a plausible subset, and (3) *data analysis* to link the variation in the output measure to some of the inputs. All these analyses have different tools to aid a Six Sigma project team.

Tools for Process Analysis

There are many tools for process analysis, more so than for any other aspect of Six Sigma because business processes lie at the heart of any organization, and identifying and analyzing these predates Six Sigma. As already mentioned, we should use any approach with which we are already comfortable. However, two tools closely associated with Six Sigma are the *cause-and-effect* (C&E) matrix and *failure-mode-and-effects analysis* (FMEA). Another important tool is *value-stream analysis* that comes from Lean Manufacturing.

CAUSE-AND-EFFECT MATRIX

The C&E matrix is one of the basic tools of any Six Sigma project we can use in phases in addition to Analyze. It is a systematic way to quantify the impact of each step in the current process on customer requirements, as a way to prioritize underlying problems and identify their causes.

There are many variants of this matrix, but a simple one consists of a single table (see Figure 7-9). In the first column, we list each process step. In the next, we list all of the inputs for the particular process step. The remaining columns represent customer requirements weighted on a scale of 1 to 10 according to how important each requirement is to that customer. The customer may provide these weightings, or team members may estimate them based on their own perceptions of the customer.

In these columns, we then rate the perceived effect each step has on each requirement, also on a scale from 1 to 10. Finally, the total score for each step, in the far right column, is the total of the scores weighted by the importance each requirement has to the customer. Thus, the higher the total, the greater the impact the process step has on the customer's requirements. The greater the overall total score, the greater is the perceived impact of the whole process on the customer.

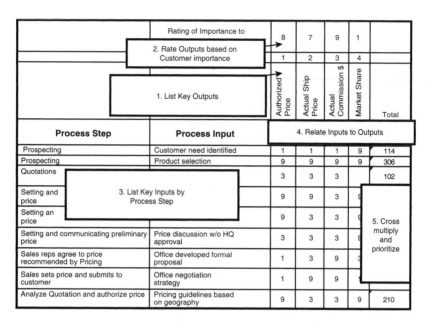

Figure 7-9   Example of a cause-and-effect (C&E) matrix

FAILURE-MODES-AND-EFFECTS ANALYSIS

FMEA is another way to understand how processes can "fail" in the sense of producing defective output. FMEA enhances the effectiveness in prioritizing issues to fix using a multifunctional team that rates problems on how severe the impact of an occurrence is ("severity"), how often it occurs ("occurrence"), and how easy it is to detect in real time ("detectability") (see Figure 7-10).

FMEA identifies potential risks to the process performance. It identifies prioritized actions to reduce risk as well as a basis for troubleshooting. Team members complete the inputs and rate severity, occurrence, and detection values. The outputs are a prioritized list of actions to take to reduce risk, identifying who does what and when. FMEA is also used in the Improve phase to figure out which of the possible improvements should be recommended.

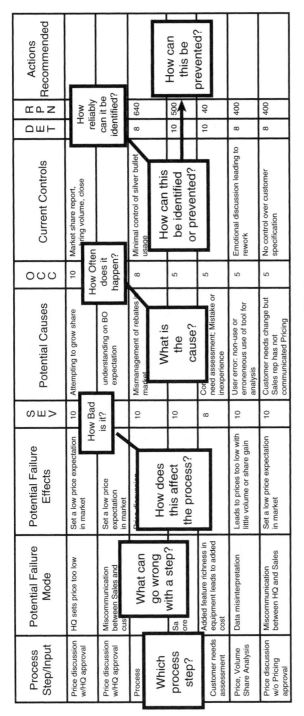

Figure 7-10   Example of FMEA

In one company, the process map showed that Sales reps could and sometimes did commit to low prices to the customer without approval from the Pricing group. The review team working on the C&E concluded this was a high-priority problem. The FMEA reflected that the problem rated high in severity and moderately high on occurrence—in the absence of control, occurrence could go up. More disturbing was that the problem was not able to be detected easily—how would someone determine whether the customer was asking for a low price or if the salesperson offered one as an enticement to close a deal. Therefore, the review team recognized that precluding this it was something to aim for in the longer term rather than address right away.

VALUE-STREAM ANALYSIS

Value-stream analysis is a core part of Lean Manufacturing that has at its focus identifying those steps that add value and those that do not, with the eventual goal of helping to eliminate waste. A value-adding activity in the process is one that transforms or shapes raw material or information to meet customer requirements. For pricing processes, this definition may seem too abstract, but it still applies. The transformation applies to information in the form of status—a proposed price turns into an approved price that in turn changes into an invoiced price. The customer in this case may be the organization's customer, but more likely it would be Sales, Marketing, Finance, or senior management. One could also argue that pricing processes to check or control prices are not value-adding but value-enabling. However, this is splitting hairs because eventually pricing processes add to the bottom line.

Value-stream analysis could be quite useful in understanding and reducing the time it takes for Pricing to respond to salespersons' requests for price approvals. Note that the goal with value-stream analysis is decreasing time or improving the rate rather than reducing variability, the aim of Six Sigma projects. However, in many situations, reducing waste and reducing variability go hand-in-hand.

The fact that we have identified activities as non-value-adding does not mean we can eliminate them: These may pertain to inspection or control, setup in the form of research on previous sales to the same customer in the particular region, or time to contact a senior manager for approval because the discount is above the discretion of the Pricing manager. However, failures whether external (for example, a customer finds out that the invoiced price is more than the offered price) or internal (invoiced price is lower than the approved price) are non-value-adding activities that can and should be targeted. The same applies to delays. Not only does eliminating failures and delays reduce the overall time but also reduces the variability in the output measure that shows up as defects. This is why Lean and Six Sigma (and Six Sigma Pricing) can work together well as Lean Six Sigma.

Tools for Root-Cause Analysis

A *fishbone diagram* is quite useful in graphically showing the possible first-level causes of a problem or questions arising from the process analysis. Besides showing the possible reasons, a fishbone diagram also shows possible underlying causes behind the first-level reasons. These are second-level causes, and we can have causes of these at lower levels as well. The head of the fish skeleton is the main question or problem, and the bones sticking out from the backbone of the fish are first-level causes. These bones may have their own second-level causes and so on.

Optionally, we can use categories of first-level causes to initiate discussion in the brainstorming sessions or otherwise compile first-level causes. For manufacturing projects, these categories may be, for instance, Machine, Methods, Measurement, Nature, People, and Materials (see Figure 7-11).[6] For Six Sigma Pricing projects, a fishbone diagram could use stakeholder functions as categories. We may find that other categories work better in our situation. Keep in mind that the purpose of categories is to initiate discussion and to ensure that no causes at the first or second level are overlooked.

Recall that we use a fishbone diagram for root-cause analysis. Which causes among the numerous ones shown in the diagram at the first, second, and even third level are at the root of the problem? There are three ways to identify the root causes in terms of the operational ones we can chase to decrease the process variation (or, in case of a lean project, the process level in terms of service time and so on).

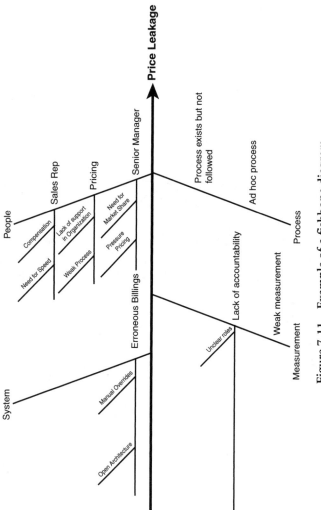

Figure 7-11 Example of a fishbone diagram

One way is to find out if any of the second-level causes show up frequently in the diagram as causing many of the first-level causes or if a first-level cause shows up in multiple categories.

A second way is to collect data on which cause is associated more frequently with the effect. For instance, we may have examined 100 "defective" invoices (with extraordinarily high discounts), and in 56 of them, we find there was no approved price—the implication being that approval was not sought. Thus one root cause is that price approvals are skipped altogether.

A third way is through voting or multi-voting whereby the team members vote as many causes "in" as they want, and the ones at the high end become the focus of discussion. We could optionally use data as in the preceding example with invoices if we have access to it. After all, fact-and-data-based reasoning is core to Six Sigma philosophy, and this principle should be used in all analyses within Six Sigma. Voting sheds light on which causes are better to pursue to improve the process and helps build consensus. In the previous invoice example, it may well emerge that the cause underlying skipping price approvals is excessive turnaround times for these requests.

Tools For Data Analysis

For data we have already compiled, we use different statistical tests depending on the type of data. A simple guide to the choice of techniques is as follows: When the output Y is continuous use *multiple regression* and *scatter plots* when all the inputs are continuous and use analysis of variance, or *ANOVA,* when all the inputs are discrete. When the output is discrete, use cross-tabulation (and the associated chi-square statistics) when the inputs are also discrete and use *logit regression* when the inputs are continuous (see Table 7-1).

The tools we will most likely use in a Six Sigma Pricing project are ANOVA and scatter plots (and regression) because the output measure, for example, discount off list, will likely be continuous. We describe these below.

Table 7-1   Statistical Technique to Use Depending on Type of X and Y
Variables

	Discrete X	Continuous X
Discrete Y	Cross-tabulation, Chi-square	Logit regression
Continuous Y	ANOVA	Multiple Regression Scatter Slots

ANOVA

ANOVA is a general-purpose tool that checks whether the average output is the same across different "populations" segmented by different levels of the input measures. We could use ANOVA to test whether different sales regions have the same average discounts—here *sales region* have four different settings: (1) North America (2) Europe and Middle East, (3) Far East, and (4) South America. The sales region is the discrete X, and the discount level off the list price is the continuous Y. Such straightforward testing is called a *one-way ANOVA*: We segment the population on the basis of the different settings of one input measure at a time, for example separating transactions from the four different regions when "region" is selected as the input measure to study.

The benefit of such testing is to find out whether discount levels depend on regions. An ANOVA test may indicate that the difference between regions is not statistically significant, in which case it would be convenient to have the same discount guidelines for all four regions. If, however, ANOVA indicates that not all four regions are the same, we may do root-cause analysis to check for different competitive pressures in different regions and have different guidelines.

Such a test can also be useful to find out whether or not we should offer a global price to our global customers. For instance, if sales regions are different according to ANOVA tests of transactions data, offering a single global price (or discount) means we will be offering discounts to these customers larger than what the competitive pressure in the different regions warrants. We can always suggest our global customers to compare prices of the same goods on Amazon.com for the U.S. market and Amazon.co.uk for the UK market and amaze themselves by the large differential in prices due to different competitive pressures in the two countries!

Suppose we had another input measure, invoice size, coded such that it has three settings, Small/Medium/Large. We could do a one-way ANOVA on this invoice size as well by comparing the average discount for the three populations of transactions corresponding to the three settings. Moreover, we could do a two-way ANOVA that compares the 12 different settings for all combinations of sales region and invoice size. This is the interaction effect that we spoke of earlier in DOE. It is useful to uncover patterns of discounts at a finer granularity than that afforded by the one-way tests.

SCATTER PLOTS

Scatter plots are commonly found in most spreadsheet packages and are extremely useful when both the input measure X and the output measure Y are continuous. (We can use these, albeit with less effect, when X is discrete.[7]) Scatter plots can help form intuition when there are easily discernible patterns in the data connecting X and Y.

On the other hand, a pattern, whether cigar-shaped or other, does not indicate we have found a root cause. All we know is that the two measures are indicated as having a link based on the data that has been collected. This link does not always imply causation, for it may be that a different cause affects them both.

This is important to understand because our purpose of finding causes is to identify things we can measure and control, thereby controlling the variation in the output measure.

If these patterns are cigar-shaped, that is, clouds around straight lines, then and only then, can we use some other statistics such as correlation analysis and regression analysis. Correlation tells us when there is a straight-line relationship between two measures—when Y goes up as X goes up, it is called positive correlation, and when Y goes down as X goes up, it is called negative correlation. When there is no effect on Y as X goes up, we have zero correlation.

Incidentally, when our (discrete) data comprises ranks for both X and Y, we can use correlation to indicate how the two ranks are linked with each other, positively or negatively. Even when both X and Y are continuous, rank-order correlation (converting both sets of data to their respective ranks and then doing correlation) can be quite useful because the computations do not get distorted by extreme values or by the distribution of the data for either variable.

REGRESSION ANALYSIS
Regression analysis is the statistical equivalent of drawing a straight line through the points and listing the parameters of this straight line, called regression coefficients. The coefficient corresponding to any of the X's shows how much Y is expected to change (on average) with a unit change in the value of X. As such, it can be quite useful. Moreover, the technique also shows whether the coefficient is worthwhile using at all. The results show whether the coefficient is significantly different from zero—if it is not, there is no point using it.

There are many pitfalls regarding regression besides the fact we cannot and should not use it unless all our variables are continuous. Regression will always draw a straight line regardless of whether or not there is any straight-line pattern in the data, so we should always check the presence of such patterns with a scatter plot first. It is also sensitive to the presence of outliers, oddball points that are far from the other points. Therefore, we need to scrub the data carefully in order to use regression. ANOVA is a much more robust technique but does not provide the kind of detailed and useful information we get from regression. In any case, the two techniques apply to different types of input data.

7.5 Tools for the Improve Phase

When using tools for the Improve phase, keep in mind that the primary purpose of these tools is to communicate and thus help in building a shared understanding and consensus. If you can achieve that in some other way, use that way instead. Consensus and management buy-in at this phase is crucial because success of the implementation or even whether the implementation gets off the ground depends on these.

A simple tool to use is the *prioritization matrix*, which is similar to the cause-and-effect matrix for a group exercise. The real purpose of this matrix is to build consensus and a shared understanding among the team members from different functions. We can list all the solutions to pursue in rows and the different criteria with weights (1-10) in the columns. These criteria could include ease of implementation, speed of implementation, and impact on customer requirement. Each table entry would reflect how well the solution in the row would meet the particular criterion. We then score each solution along the row by summing up the table entry scores along the row weighted by the respective criteria weight.

A simpler version of the prioritization matrix is the *payoff matrix* with business impact on the vertical axis and ease of implementation or effort on the horizontal axis. All solutions under consideration can be scored on both axes between 1 and 10 using a team exercise, possibly with the management committee overseeing the project, called the Project Steering Committee. Then the prioritization is visual with solutions that have a higher perceived impact and higher ease of implementation (or lower effort) getting a higher priority than other solutions. Note that with a prioritization matrix we can use any number of criteria, whereas with the payoff matrix, we are limited to two criteria.

Another tool for highlighting the risks associated with implementation is the FMEA, or failure-mode-and-effects analysis that we had discussed before in process analysis within the Analyze phase. In the present context, the team uses FMEA to understand and to convey to the Steering Committee how the implementation of the proposed solutions can fail rather than how the existing process fails, as we saw before. The main causes of failure are that the new process is not followed or that management does not buy into the proposed solutions and therefore does not follow up to ensure implementation. Therefore, it is important to bring these potential failures up in review meetings before implementation is to begin. FMEA provides a way to convey these risks in a comprehensive and apolitical manner.

In this phase, we use tools that help monitor the reduction in defects and whether the recommended and agreed-upon steps are actually being carried out.

"To-Be" Process Map

This process map should have the same level of detail as the "as-is" process map in the Measure phase to allow for easy comparison. Moreover, it should reflect the controls that team members have devised and agreed to with the Steering Committee of the project.

7.6 Tools for the Control Phase

The use of the tools should be in the hand-off document that ends the "design" part of the project before implementation begins.[8]

Control Charts

Control charts for measures show what measures are being "controlled" and for which data is being collected and how. A control chart has upper and lower control limits to indicate whether the process variability for the measure chosen is satisfactory. If a number of successive points are consistently higher than the upper control limit or lower than the lower control limit, we can say that the process is "out-of-control." A control chart without limits is called a *run chart*, which is used to indicate *trends* and *shifts* in the level of the process measure.[9]

For instance, a control chart can be used to show discount data from invoices sampled randomly from all regions each month. Control charts are graphs over time: For pricing, the time bin may be a week or a four-week month (or calendar month). The metric to track may be the number of defectively priced invoices (based on an agreed upon definition of defective) by region, the average discount level weighted by invoice size for all invoices in the period corresponding to the bin, or the use of exception codes (see the next section) by personnel or by region.

Exception Codes

Exception codes are quite useful for pricing processes to control the number of exceptions without imposing strict process controls that do not allow any flexibility. The database with invoices gets additional fields that indicate why a workaround was needed and who initiated it or authorized it. Pricing processes cannot have the rigidity of assembly line processes with the exact same process followed for every widget manufactured. These processes will always have exceptions where a process shortcut or a one-off workaround is warranted. The purpose of exception codes is to check how often this takes place and whether the personnel or regions initiating such exceptions tend to be the same over time. The fact that someone is tracking workarounds itself can be a deterrent, but pricing processes do need the flexibility and exception codes provide that while still providing control.

Scorecards

Scorecards of various shapes and hues are essentially control tools. The breadth of the scorecard depends on what is being controlled—the *Balanced Scorecard*, for instance, aims to check the direction of the entire organization.[10] The success of scorecards is to select a limited number of measures that together describe all the attributes of interest of the process in question. Visual descriptions include using red-amber-green labels to indicate what is within control and what is not. In particular, for implementation efforts we can use a scorecard to track how many people have been trained in the new process or to track the IT effort to modify the data fields to capture exception codes.

7.7 Summary

Each phase of a Six Sigma project has a set of tools intended to help achieve the goal for that phase. In the Define phase, we seek to identify the problem and its magnitude in the context of a particular process, so tools for displaying descriptive statistics with bar charts, pie charts, or frequency diagrams, along with preliminary analysis by way of a SIPOC process chart, is quite useful.

In Measure, we seek to describe the process in more detail and to gather data about it as well as to decide which part of the process is worth focusing on for improvement. The same tools used in Define earlier as well as cause-and-effects diagrams and FMEA are quite useful. In addition, we need to make templates to collect process-specific data in terms of quantified inputs (X's) and quantified output (Y).

The third phase, Analyze, endeavors to find the reasons for variation in the output and consequently the generation of defects. We do so in any of three ways, all of which have their specific tools. One way is process analysis for which we use the details of the current process. The second is root-cause analysis in which we try to find underlying causes for failure in a particular step or the entire process. The third is data analysis whereby we try to relate the X's to the Y using tools such as cross-tabulations, multiple regression, and ANOVA to determine how the output depends on each of the inputs.

In the Improve phase, we start with a long list of improvements, so we need tools such as FMEA or a prioritization matrix to help us prioritize the changes we want to recommend.

Finally, for Control, we have tools that help monitor the reduction in defects and whether the recommended and agreed upon steps are actually being carried out. Tracking can be achieved through control charts taken from statistical process control (SPC) at one extreme and scorecards for senior managers at the other. Either way, the purpose of these should be to ensure these are part of planning and useful for continuous improvement and future projects.

Part III

Doing a Six Sigma Pricing Project

8

SELECTING A SIX SIGMA PRICING PROJECT

Decide what you want, decide what you are willing to exchange for it. Establish your priorities and go to work.

—*H. L. Hunt*

8.1 Introduction

One important reason Six Sigma is different from its predecessors in regard to quality management is that only those projects that provide good value for the effort are meant to be taken up. Still, companies that make Six Sigma training or an implemented project a requirement for promotion or bonus risk employees picking up mundane projects just to "tick the box."

Six Sigma requires the selection of projects to be based on a solid business cases to ensure that the projects will have economic value. In this chapter, we outline various processes that generally fall under the area of Six Sigma Pricing and provide some tools to help bring about consensus. Alternatively, you may already have some procedures in your company to select projects, and you could use those procedures instead to build on consensus.

Unless there is a "burning platform," it is difficult to expect that there would be any interest in starting a pricing project, whether or not it uses Six Sigma. Therefore, the involved parties must acknowledge that price must be improved or at least prevented from deteriorating further and that improvement of some pricing-related processes is one way to do it. The step following such acknowledgement is selecting the processes the team wants to use.

Selecting the "right" project in pricing improves its chances for success. Executive support at the outset, during the project, during implementation, and during adoption of the revised processes is critical because of the different functions pulling in different directions regarding pricing. Especially relevant is the involvement, if not complete agreement, of Sales executives. The project team should choose a scope that is visible, realistic, and manageable. Moreover, the scope should be broad enough to clearly show meaningful benefit for multiple stakeholders and structured well enough to get the acquiescence, if not whole-hearted support of all stakeholders, including Sales, even before convincing hard evidence is available.

Senior managers are likely to sponsor projects that support the company's strategic plan or address the "burning platform" issues facing the business consistent with the goals set by senior managers. These high-level goals need to be translated into measurable objectives at a functional level for managers to execute.

Next, we discuss the following elements that are necessary for building consensus around project selection:

- Business objectives and key performance metrics
- Problem areas
- Project prioritization
- Leadership support

Business Objectives and Key Performance Metrics

Like any other successful project, a Six Sigma Pricing project should support key business objectives to get upper management commitment. Any improvement should be measurable through key performance metrics. This means understanding business objectives and knowing which metrics can be affected. In establishing key business objectives, companies generally set aggressive agendas in the form of market share or sales growth, increasing profitability while maintaining market share, launching innovative products, or cutting operational costs, say, by expanding manufacturing plants in China and outsourcing back office operations to India.

Although every company seeks (or should seek) long-term profitability as its key objective, it is not always clear how to trade off sales growth against growth in (near-term) profits. Consider computer manufacturer Dell. In Dell's case, one of their critical objectives must be price improvement. The chief executive, Kevin B. Rollins,[1] said in August 2006 that the company had cut prices "too aggressively" in a number of markets to win market share, which hurt its profitability. "We didn't do a good job of it," he said. Investors were also frustrated, with Dell shares dropping more than 5% in extended trading after the earnings report. Dell saw that net income dropped 51% to $502 million from $1.02 billion a year earlier. Rather than continuing to increase market share at the expense of losing price, Dell chose to improve prices. Their earnings release in November 2006[2] showed the net income for the third quarter at $677 million, up 11.7% from the previous year, and revenue was up 3.4% to $14.4 billion. Investors looked upon this favorably and pushed shares up sharply. Still, the loss in profits due to price deterioration may have been a contributing factor in Michael Dell taking back the helm of the company.[3]

Problem Areas

After pricing has been identified as a critical area of improvement, managers need to identify causes before they can start fixing problems. Imagine how quickly the managers at Dell must have had to deal with the situation under intense pressure from Wall Street. This would require cross-functional teams of stakeholders to brainstorm around questions from their internal and external environment similar to the ones listed below that we have categorized by function for ease of presentation although many issues span multiple functions:

Customer Service

1. Are customers complaining about invoicing problems regularly?

2. What kind of problems do our customer service representatives find when taking orders? How often?

IT

1. Are there known computer- or program-related problems affecting the productivity of Sales or Pricing personnel?

2. Are there discount codes in the quotation system that are active past their expiration dates? Can and do employees work around system controls with manual overrides without proper justification?

3. Is there a single database with the list price, approved or system-generated, and the invoice price?

4. Is it clear who has access to what regarding prices on the system? Was the security and access actually implemented in the system?

5. Are quotes actually valid for only the period stated on the quote? Can a customer/salesperson use a quote that expired two years ago to make a purchase now?

Senior Management

1. How are we doing on realizing price? Are we happy with the results?

2. Are competitive prices lower or higher than ours?

3. Are there consistent complaints about channel conflict from distributors or retailers?

4. Are there many people outside the Pricing department who have the "final" authority over pricing?

5. Is contract compliance satisfactory? How do we currently ensure compliance with customer contracts in regard to volume and pricing?

6. What am I most concerned about at the end of the period?

7. What process seems always broken? What do we seem to fix over and over and over again? Is this particular to a business line, sales region, Marketing office, Pricing office?

8. Where do personnel from Pricing, Sales, Marketing, or Customer Service take the path of least resistance rather than strive for a solution? Which processes have band-aids or short-cuts?

9. What gives me a headache?

Pricing

1. What does Pricing try to fix everyday? Which fires do personnel fight everyday at different levels?

2. Are there contracts that are being violated by price offers that are lower than those specified by the contract?

3. Is the staff turnover in Pricing in any world region greater than expected?

4. Do Pricing personnel have clear guidelines?

5. Are people able to override system controls to get around established rules for discounts?

6. For which people/sales regions/business lines have the most pricing-related issues?

7. What Pricing/Marketing office do we need to check on routinely?

8. What work instructions do we need to reinforce in different pricing processes?

9. What function, including IT, does Pricing need to contact routinely for problem solving?

10. Are there too many "unique" situations when it comes to certain customers in any industry or region asking for discounts? Are there rules established for these exceptions?

11. Is there a difference between what pricing processes require and what has been implemented in the company's enterprise resource planning (ERP) or other transaction system?

12. What takes too long? Are responses to price approvals quickly turned over?

Sales

1. What do Sales personnel complain about the most in regard to Pricing?

2. What Sales office do we need to check on routinely?

Project Prioritization and Selection

Inter-functional brainstorming sessions draw participants into a constructive discussion even though the functional agendas and incentives differ. We have experienced the awe expressed by participants, including employees who have been at a company for a long time, as they begin to understand the complexity of pricing practices and processes in their companies. The number and the diversity of issues that come up as listed here reflect this complexity. While it is beneficial for participants to speak of their problems and propose ideas for fixing them, one concern is finding a starting point among the daunting list of 50–60 things to fix.

Another question is whether all teams would pull in the same direction to fix any chosen problem given the different functional and individual agendas. In general, the answer is no, even though cross-functional players can compromise on individual issues to enable a short-term fix. However, this may not lead to sustainable improvement without the team first building a foundation of similar motivation on all sides.

The moderator of the brainstorming session should encourage the participants to group their problems and issues into common themes such as, strategy-related, process-related, people-related, and so on, rather than by function (as we showed above). Another way would be to arrange these by process. Either way, the moderator helps draw the participants out of their respective functional silos into understanding the bigger picture.

The brainstorming team can objectively start applying criteria for prioritization. Such criteria can be return-on-investment (ROI) or relative benefit, resources required or overall cost of execution, time-to-market, ease of execution, and urgency. The type of resources and their quantity may play a part in the selection of a project. Sometimes capital expenditure may also be needed although Six Sigma Pricing projects themselves should not be capital-intensive. For example, some software or programming may be required to monitor prices or to put blocks on ridiculously low prices or prices that are below approved prices. Once the baseline data has been established, the financial value of the project must be established. Eventually, every project must be able to stand scrutiny regarding the question of resources—would the time and money be better spent on other projects?

Expected time to complete a project is also a useful criterion. That way even if the project is not successful or the recommendations cannot be implemented for political reasons, effort can shift to other projects that are more feasible. In addition, if the project can be implemented earlier, benefits can be obtained sooner. Our recommendation is that a duration of 10 to 12 weeks for many Six Sigma Pricing projects is a good benchmark between the start and the final presentation with recommendations—with a similar duration for implementation. Projects that take longer than this may either drift into oblivion, or their recommendations may be so wide-ranging that they cannot be implemented. These are Green-Belt level projects in Six Sigma terms. Later, with more experience, you can try Black-Belt projects of 20 to 30 weeks or even longer. As with many other things, but more so with Six Sigma Pricing projects, walking before running is a good idea.

Besides quantifiable or "hard" benefits, projects can have benefits that are tangible but soft or even pointless to quantify in dollar terms. Examples of such "soft" benefits are

- Time-to-market (new products, new prices, price changes)
- Shorter cycle time for quoting and ordering
- Simplification and standardization of processes
- Reduction in emotion in interfunction interactions
- Role clarification
- Customer satisfaction

There are several tools to help prioritize and select projects. The basic premise of these tools is building consensus among the team and ensuring senior management buy-in. A few of the better known tools for project selection are the typical tools used in Six Sigma projects: a cause-and-effect (C&E) matrix, consecutive filters, and stakeholder analysis, which were discussed in detail in Chapter 7, "Tools for Six Sigma." However, we mention these again here in the context of project selection.

The C&E matrix is a general-purpose method used in different phases of any Six Sigma project. Although we do not really have "causes" and "effects" when selecting projects, we can use the matrix to estimate how much each project ranks according to different criteria or key business objectives that have different weights. We can then shortlist or order projects based on the total scores they get across. The benefit of such a tool lies in helping build a consensus rather than getting the right "scores." Indeed, you may well find that after the dust settles, the consensus view on which projects to select may be different from those indicated by individual scores.

Using consecutive filters is a simpler approach entailing the application of criteria or "filters" sequentially to iteratively shortlist projects when there are many competing ideas. The benefit of doing so is that as a focus group, all the people can focus on one criterion at a time. However, such an approach does not allow trade-offs. Moreover, the short list produced may depend on the sequence of applying the filters, which makes the sequence prone to gaming.

Stakeholder analysis is a simple tool to share views about different stakeholders on two dimensions: (1) their power to support a project or initiative and (2) their interest in supporting the project or initiative (see Chapter 7, "Tools for Six Sigma"). The analysis can be used to rank projects along the two dimensions as well: Projects whose total scores for the main stakeholders are high on both dimensions should rank higher than those that are lower, at least from the viewpoint of feasibility.

Leadership Support

Projects with leadership support, especially in a contention-prone area like pricing, have a higher chance of being implemented and therefore of being successful. There may be some gaming associated with which project to select first. The ideal situation is to have senior managers from different functions involved in selecting the projects, with feasibility of implementation being discussed openly. There is always temptation to select ambitious projects that promise huge benefits but are unlikely to be implemented.

8.2 Acme

Going back to our case study (Chapter 3, "Case Study—Pricing Operations and Six Sigma Pricing"), Acme had more than one pricing function within each division—one reporting to Marketing and the other to Sales. The processes used by the two pricing groups were completely different, although they shared a significant part of the company's customer base. The Marketing division had hired a Pricing manager, hoping to develop standardized pricing processes for the entire company.

However, functional agendas were too strong for any effort for process standardization or improvement to bear fruit. Sales personnel wanted flexibility on discounts, while product managers wanted authority because they were responsible for P&L. Different analyses had delineated the benefits pricing improvement could bring the company, but these efforts did not get critical attention. Part of the reason was quite practical: No one wanted a situation where price improvements led to lost market share, analyses notwithstanding. It was not until the company faced significant unplanned cost increases that the senior management seriously considered price improvement.

Specifically, there was a lot of noise and emotion surrounding the process for approving discounts. On one hand was the Sales team that resented the Pricing team for holding them back on extending discounts when they felt they had the best understanding of the customers' needs. On the other hand was Pricing, who felt that Sales already had enough flexibility but still tended to give in easily without selling the customers on the value of the product. Acme had a poor track record of realizing gains from list price increases it had announced in the past.

When hit by unprecedented raw material inflation, Acme had no choice but to focus on price to cover unplanned incremental costs. The Pricing manager asked a Six Sigma Blackbelt to moderate a brainstorm session between representatives from Sales, Pricing, Manufacturing, and Product Management. The discussion points were recorded on flipcharts—we list these to show the number and variety of issues (some came up repeatedly), arranged by theme for ease of reading (the moderator suggested a different grouping, as discussed later):

Price approval process

1. Too many handoffs in the discount approval process.
2. Too much time is taken by Pricing analysts to approve.
3. The discount process is very manual, needs to be automated.
4. Too much time taken up in creating and analyzing facts.
5. Sales does not provide required information, wastes time in the process.
6. The process for accessing price/cost information takes too long.

7. Quotes are not at market price initially therefore ongoing debate.
8. Competitive analysis is weak.
9. Where is competitive pricing data?
10. Discount decisions are based on manufacturing cost not market price.
11. Poor visibility to cost data for Sales—need it early in process.
12. No value selling, Sales gives in on price quickly.

Organizational and interfunction issues

1. Disconnect between incentives and decisions.
2. Inconsistent application of margin thresholds (as discount criteria).
3. Too many silos—not enough delegation.
4. Multiple owners in process.
5. No clear owner—lack of defined roles.
6. Too many decision makers.
7. Manufacturing is not included in the pricing decision.
8. Sales force is not trained in price negotiation.
9. Limited product manager involvement in concessions process.

General issues related to pricing operations

1. Metrics are non-existent.
2. Discount goals not linked to business goals.
3. Transfer pricing is not clear.
4. Variation in the pricing process is high.
5. What is the ongoing process for monitoring the pricing process?
6. Do you do regular price reviews? How often? Who?
7. There are price negotiations internal and external to the company.
8. What is the appropriate way to use pricing as a tool to balance factory load?

General issues related to pricing strategy and processes

1. Need to consider channel conflict.
2. Need to sell based on value for customer, not manufacturing cost.
3. Competitive data is not collected systematically.
4. Product lifecycle pricing—how do we price new products?
5. How do we do price/value mapping?
6. How do you position your pricing strategy relative to price/volume/share?
7. If you are not a market leader, what pricing strategy do you use?
8. How do we do competitive analysis ... how should we look at markets and capacity?
9. How do we package our offerings to optimize features?

Communication

1. Multiple media used for communication, not sure where to look.
2. Decision making information is not shared.
3. No standard channel for notifying customer.
4. Lack of documented standardized process.

The discussion underscored conflicting objectives of the functional teams. For instance, one team desired speedy response to requests for additional discounts for closing deals quickly to generate more business overall—certainly a good objective. In contrast, another asked for in-depth competitive price analysis, value-selling when the Sales team just wanted greater flexibility in offering discounts. The team had to prioritize actions based on a lot of unstructured commentary. The project manager moderating the brainstorm constantly reminded the participants of the business priorities related to the need for price improvement.

The Blackbelt asked the team to opt for one of the four potential directions as the best way to fix many problems:

1. Adopt a different pricing strategy
2. Improve pricing process and policies
3. Improve analytical tools and processes
4. Focus on compliance by defining clear responsibilities and incentives

He also asked the participants to collectively agree on a single choice to categorize each brainstormed item. (Recall that the previous categorization was just for ease of reading.) Next, the team had to agree on rating how each idea affected the desired results sought by their "customer," a senior manager at Acme who wanted price improvement. The desired results and therefore criteria were

1. Potential ROI
2. Ease of execution
3. Ability to leverage across the entire business

The team rated the desired outputs equally after agreeing that the senior manager was equally interested in all three (this meant equal weights for the three criteria). After this, the team rated each process input in relation to output in order to fill the rest of the C&E spreadsheet. Once again, the moderator directed the team to agree on a single score for each entry. After the team did this, they calculated total scores and displayed the items in descending order (see Figure 8-1).

The pricing manager further reviewed the list of issues that came up in the brainstorming session. While issues related to "Adopt a different pricing strategy" had scored some of the highest individual total scores, "Improve pricing process and policies" as a category dominated the Pareto chart, showing which of the four directions or projects would fix more problems (see Figure 8-2).

The brainstorming team had all the information they needed to come to an agreement. "Improving pricing process and policies" would alleviate most problems and bring about the much needed price realization for the company. When the senior manager, who was also general manger of one business unit at Acme, reviewed the analysis, he immediately authorized the pricing manager to fix the discounting process to increase speed and stem price leakage.

Category	Rating of Importance to Customer — Issues	Ease of Execution — 7	Potential ROI — 7	Ability to Leverage — 7	Total Score
Policies and Processes	11. Too many silos—not enough delegation	9	6	9	168
Policies and Processes	6. Too many handoffs in the discount approval process	9	6	9	168
Incentives and Responsibility	1. Quotes are not at market price initially therefore ongoing debate	3	9	9	147
Policies and Processes	22. Sales force is not trained well enough in price negotiation	3	9	9	147
Pricing Strategy	25. How do we build consensus about our pricing strategy?	3	9	9	147
Analytical Tools	59. We don't fully understand our pricing strategy?	3	9	9	147
Analytical Tools	62. Too much time taken by Pricing analysts	1	9	9	133
Policies and Processes	7. The discount process is very manual, needs to be automated	3	6	9	126
Policies and Processes	9. The discount process is very manual, needs to be automated	3	6	9	126
Policies and Processes	13. Disconnect between incentives and decisions	3	6	9	126
Pricing Strategy	14. Inconsistent application of margin thresholds	3	6	9	126
Policies and Processes	26. Sales do not provide required information, wastes time in the process	6	3	9	126
Policies and Processes	10. Multiple media used for communication, not sure where to look	3	6	9	126
Analytical Tools	54. Lack of a consolidated database: price levels, price trends over time, etc.	3	6	9	126
Policies and Processes	12. Too much time creating and analyzing facts	3	3	9	105
Incentives Responsibility	29. Unclear who's responsible for pricing—different aspects handled by different people	3	6	6	105
Analytical Tools	57. Most data is created manually	3	3	6	84

Figure 8-1 Project selection at Acme using a C&E matrix (sampling of items from a larger matrix)

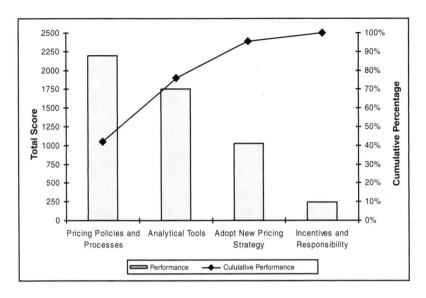

Figure 8-2   Pareto chart showing which direction
or projects would fix most problems

8.3 Summary

Multi-functional teams or committees charged with finding ways to improve price processes need to follow a systemic process using simple tools to communicate and share information because of the need to develop consensus. One, the members of such a team should brainstorm and list all issues. Two, they should agree on their understanding of senior management's priorities. Three, they should categorize these issues into broad directions or initiatives. Four, they should use a tool such as the C&E matrix to help understand the trade-offs and identify initiatives that have the highest potential impact in terms of the team's understanding of senior management's priorities. Five, they can present the results of their analysis to senior management to specify or scope specific projects. This way the selection process starts building upon a foundation of cross-functional agreement, if not full consensus, and buy-in from senior management.

9

DEFINE PHASE

The greatest challenge to any thinker is stating the problem in a way that will allow a solution.

—*Bertrand Russell (1872–1970)*

9.1 Introduction

The Define phase includes identifying a process for improvement and making a sales pitch to the management for project approval. As such, the important output of this phase is a scope, a time line, expected improvement in numbers—sometimes only a wild guess—and other benefits. The deliverables must be clearly defined, as they were, for instance, for Acme's Six Sigma Pricing project. We can think of the three components of Define as "tollgates" needed for completing this phase: *the charter, customer requirements,* and a *high-level process map.*[1]

The eventual purpose is to obtain approval from a diverse group of stakeholders and to ensure that the entire team and the Steering Committee agree on what to expect from the project. This is something to keep in mind when thinking about the three components needed to complete this phase of a Six Sigma Pricing project. After all, as with any proposal, we have to show we are aware not only of the problem but also of the context in terms of customer requirements and the high-level process.

9.2 The Charter

The charter is the bulk of the Define documentation that can range from a single slide presentation to a bundle of detailed pages. If the company already has a Six Sigma program, we may be better off sticking with the existing approach and the vocabulary that is already in place. Still, it is worth discussing the purpose of the Define phase and the key elements:

Definition of Defect

First, we have to identify and define what the defect is. At the same time we have to identify and quantify the problem (see section "A Numerical

---

150   SIX SIGMA PRICING

Definition of the Problem" that follows). This is why this stage of Six Sigma is called "Define."

Identifying or defining the defect is crucial because this establishes how we will measure success and what process we will improve. Moreover, a transaction may be defective in many ways with different processes or subprocesses contributing to the problem. There may be invoicing problems in addition to the price being too low, or the terms may not match with the contract—or all of the above. So we also have to select the type of the defect we want to decrease rather than try to correct all problems all at once, even though it may sound attractive to tackle all the problems right away.

Recalling Six Sigma's roots in manufacturing, we can make an analogy: Just as a poor manufacturing process produces defective widgets that could be faulty in many ways, a bad pricing process can produce defective prices, defective contracts, or responses with excessive turnaround times to salespersons' requests for price approval. The source of the defect in either case is variation in process quality, which is why we can use Six Sigma whether it is in manufacturing widgets or pricing them.

For instance, a defect may be a transaction whose price is too low, say, with a discount of more than 50% off the list. It may also be a poorly worded contract that can result in low prices in the long run. The process we are trying to improve—transaction price setting or contract writing—should be a repeated process that will produce nondefective or defective items in the future, whether these are transaction prices or contracts. Eventually, we are trying to control the number of defects.

The point of view is important. From a salesperson's view, a slow response from Pricing on a price-approval request could mean a loss in sales: Thus a response time that is greater than, say eight hours, is a "defect." Pricing in any company has a number of stakeholders, so there is going to be long list of "defects" depending on the viewpoint, so getting to agree on which defect to address can be a challenge.

Unlike most manufacturing or service situations, with pricing situations, we may find that by decreasing the number of defects of one type we increase those of another. For instance, we could eventually reduce excessively high discounts on transactions by requiring a more detailed and strictly enforced price-approval process. This, however, could mean even longer turnaround times of salespersons' requests for price approval from Pricing, potential loss of sales for the company, and possibly a worse bottom line than before the recommendations from the Six Sigma project were implemented. This would require the recently implemented process changes to be rolled back. Therefore, when going after one type of defect, we will find that with pricing we have to take other types of defects into account and ensure that these do not worsen because of the process changes we are recommending. For pricing projects, even successful projects may get rolled back.

A Numerical Definition of the Problem

A useful requirement for Define is to describe the "problem" quantitatively. This could be as simple as writing the number of defects per so many occurrences. This is where the term *defects per million opportunities* (DPMO) comes in. For manufacturing in a company like Motorola, a few million chips is not a large number. However, for pricing, instead of per million we could have per thousand or even per hundred—after all, we may not have a few million open contracts to be able to state the number of defective contracts among a million of them!

Alternatively, we could go a level deeper and describe some attribute of the process that produces these defects. Doing so suggests ways of handling the problem in subsequent phases.

What is measured is what gets improved. This is why in Six Sigma it is important to identify the extent of the problem numerically in terms of how often defects are occurring. This could, for instance, take the form of stating the percentage defects. "Twenty percent of our transactions in the last six months have excessively high discounts," or "More than 50 percent of our existing contracts have loopholes through which customers are able to extract discounts higher than specified in the contract." It could be that for every ten price-approval requests a salesperson in a particular region makes, four requests take more than two days. By defining the problem numerically, the benefit of process improvement is more easily quantified. Also a business case (see the "Business Case" section that follows) can be made more easily if the problem is identified numerically. In pricing, there is likely to be data available, but if not, samples or even people's opinions can be used as a proxy to identify the problem.

Goal Statement

This refers to the goal of seeking to reduce the problem by a target that is both achievable and meaningful, for instance, seeking to halve the number of transactions with prices below guidelines. Having a modest goal may be good but may not excite anyone because even if it is achieved, the benefits may be too small. On the other hand, setting up a goal that is too ambitious is also setting us up for failure especially in pricing. This is where a purist might say that we need to decrease the number of defects below three in a million, but a goal of reducing excessive discounts in 20 out of every 100 transactions to 10 defects is much more likely to succeed and still have a substantial positive impact on the bottom line.

The goal is to improve the process to a level that is somewhere between the current situation or "baseline" and an ideal or "entitlement" value that is possible but hard to achieve in the project's time frame. The next task is to estimate the benefit to the bottom line if the chosen goal were met. Ideally, this benefit should be verified or at least verifiable by Finance. We can outline both "soft" or unquantifiable benefits and "hard" or quantified benefits, but we should not use soft benefits as a crutch when estimates of the "hard" benefits are too low.

Business Case

Having selected a project earlier, we should be able to state why this particular project is worth the effort needed to do it. The tangible benefit should be clear, although there may be hard-to-quantify intangibles such as "better working environment" as well. We will have to make estimates or even "guesstimates": If excessive discounts are curtailed, not all the quotes would become orders, but how many would? We could assume that half or three-fourths of the orders will still materialize and use the lowest acceptable price on these to estimate the benefit to the bottom line. As mentioned previously, with pricing-related projects, we need to make sure that we are not worsening the bottom line by unwittingly increasing another type of defect.

How detailed and accurate do we need to be? Not very. We really need only an estimate on the low side. If this low estimate indicates that we would benefit by at least some threshold value, we can proceed. With costs, we can take a high estimate. In most Six Sigma Pricing projects, costs of implementation will be the part-time effort of the personnel involved and typically will be much lower than the potential bottom line benefit.

Scope

The scale and size of the project is a potential pitfall. If we scope the project too large, that is, we pick up a process or processes that involve many complicated steps and many people from different functions, we may potentially be setting up the project team for failure. This is especially the case with pricing projects because we will be involving people from different functions. Therefore, we have to be careful choosing which process steps to have in the scope and which ones not to include.

If the scope is "too large," it will end up getting trimmed midway through the project. Worse, the project may flounder and then be abandoned. Either way, others may see the project team as not having "done the job" even if the project is successful with the reduced scope. If the scope is "too small," the projected benefits may be too small for the project to get approval or even any notice.

Somewhere there is the "just right" Goldilocks point for a project that we can finish in two to three months working part time, possibly less than quarter-time realistically speaking. If in doubt, we should use a smaller scope when it comes to pricing—it will also be less threatening to the various stakeholders. We may have to revise the definition of defect or revise the business case after we consider the scope, but it is worth doing that.

Project Details

Besides identifying the scope, it is a good idea to outline milestones and to clarify the roles and responsibilities of the various team members. It may be worthwhile to keep pricing projects small, at least at the outset, with a few team members possibly from different functions. Identifying barriers to success is a good idea for any project. We may not be able to anticipate many problems at the outset, so focus on the barriers to success in terms of team dynamics and getting access to data. For most pricing projects, there is no shortage of data, but we need to ensure we will have access to it. As with any project being done by people within the company, we must also try to find out if the personnel on the project team would be available to invest time on the project.

9.3 Customers and Their Requirements

"Customers" for a pricing project are typically any of the various stakeholders from the different functional groups in the company: Finance, Marketing, Sales, IT, and top management. These customers will have diverse requirements that we could identify within the scope of the project so that the project has a higher chance of being approved and more than that, that the project team's recommendations get implemented. Thus the true purpose of having a slide or a paragraph about "customers and their requirements" is for the project team to be able to show that they are cognizant of the various players and their needs.

9.4 High-level Process Map

A high-level process map shows that the team knows what they are targeting regarding scope and that they have a basic understanding of the particular pricing process. How detailed should this be? "High-level" suggests it need not be very detailed. In the next phase, Measure, the team would develop a detailed process map of the "as-is" process, so here the purpose is to convey the scope. However, the analysis to support the business case may be tied to the process map, so there needs to be some detail.

9.5 Define Checklist

The following is a quick checklist to ensure we are done with this phase:

- **Problem statement**: Have we stated the problem and, in numerical terms, its extent but without stating a solution? After all, if we already have a solution, why would we be doing this project?
- **Link to business goals/customer requirements**: Have we shown that there is a link between reducing the occurrence of defects to the "customers'" requirements, that is, the business goals pertaining to the bottom line, average price, and so on?
- **Scoped properly**: Is the project scope thought through clearly in terms of being not too big and treading on lots of toes in other functional areas and not so small that the potential benefits have little impact on the bottom line?
- **Best project**: Is this the best project to be working on right now at least among the ones considered? It is not easy to figure out "best" even if everyone agrees on the criteria. However, we should be able to state that the business case is quite compelling—credible and large enough—for this project compared to that of other projects possible or in consideration.
- **Estimated benefits**: Have we figured out a rough dollar estimate of potential benefits? Have potential soft/hard benefits been identified?
- **Goal statement**: Do we have a goal statement with measurable targets, along with gap analysis on the extent to which customer/stakeholders' needs are met by the current process being targeted? Do the project's metrics align with the organization's metrics?
- **Barriers to success**: Have we identified barriers to success in regard to access to data, availability of team members, and ability to implement recommendations? Identifying these is a good thing for any project but particularly for a pricing project.
- **Approval to proceed**: Do we have the approval from the Steering Committee to proceed to the next phase?

9.6 Acme

Project selection discussion at Acme had led to the general manager of the business division giving the green light for work to begin on improving the discounting process. In the past, senior managers had dismissed occasional friction between the Pricing and Sales groups as "constructive conflict," a part of "checks and balances" in any large company. However, the sudden increases in costs of key raw materials and a lack of confidence in being able to realize price from increases in list prices had led to an interest in examining the discounting process.

Moreover, the general manager had prior plant management experience and was therefore quite comfortable with the idea of process improvement using Statistical Quality Control or Six Sigma. When the pricing manager asked the general manager to look for improvements in the discounting process using Six Sigma, he gave complete support to the idea.

The pricing manager's motivation for taking on this pricing project stemmed from wanting to improve a process that appeared to have many problems, but his motivation to use Six Sigma stemmed from the company's certification process. The company had publicly committed itself to Six Sigma methodology and had created an opportunity for nonmanufacturing personnel to get Six Sigma Green Belt certification that required training and completing a "Green Belt" project. The certification requirement was that such a project had to save or generate a minimum of $80,000 in cost savings or incremental revenues using Six Sigma within 12 months of completion. The pricing manager felt he could combine his interest in the pricing improvement process and in getting the Green Belt certification that would help his career.

The pricing manager had now had quite a bit of interaction with and encouragement from the Six Sigma Master Black Belt who had facilitated the session for identifying possible problems in the pricing processes on the transaction side. Therefore, he requested the Master Black Belt to be his mentor for this project. Although the mentor did not have detailed knowledge about pricing and pricing processes and was too senior a person in the company to be guiding "Green Belt" projects like this one, he felt that pricing was a new and potentially beneficial area that merited his attention. He accepted the role of mentor and subsequently guided the process systematically through the various phases of Six Sigma.

The project mentor's first recommendation to the pricing manager and to the rest of the project team was to develop a charter in a careful manner. The charter was to be a stand-alone document describing the following at a very minimum:

1. The business context, including the process
2. The goals of the project
3. The scope of the project
4. The resources needed for the project including the team members and any support
5. The timeline of actions or milestones
6. The benefits expected from the project

Charter Item #1: The Business Context Including the Process

The project aimed at working with the direct sales force to improve the discounting process at one business unit. This division, like others in Acme, operated in a highly negotiated environment. Sales personnel were in a disadvantaged position unless their negotiating positions were supported by price guidelines obtained through analysis of part transactions. However, there were many special cases where guidelines were not met and discounts were excessive: executive intervention, inadequate time to seek approval from pricing, and inadequate time for Pricing to analyze a particular situation.

For instance, Pricing personnel sometimes found the information provided by Sales reps to be inadequate and had to ask for additional information from them, who, being busy with other sales opportunities, could not always provide in a timely manner. On their side, Sales reps found that even after waiting for a long time and having provided all the necessary information, the approved prices were unrealistically high and did not take into consideration the special circumstances that warranted an exceptional "one-off" discount. As such, they would have to escalate the quotation request for executive intervention when they perceived the customer had "strategic" value in the long term. Thus the lack of a well-defined quotation process was leading to price degradation through excessive discounts.

Charter Item #2: Goals for the Project

In Six Sigma parlance, the goal of the project was to reduce the variance in the discount across transactions by identifying factors that the company could control to achieve the reduction in discount variance. However, it was not clear how to figure out a numerical improvement, not just to "variance reduction," but even to the eventual goal: increase in revenues due to price increases alone. Given Acme's history of price realization, different Marketing and Finance executives felt that even a 0.25% increase in incremental price increases ($500,000 for the products and pricing processes under consideration) was "too aggressive" to be achieved by means of such a project. However, they felt it may eventually be possible to achieve such an improvement through various projects and initiatives. Moreover, there were doubts about whether even the existing sales plan—revenues, margins, and price levels—for the subsequent months could be achieved. Acme, like its key competitors, used a third-party data source to check market share for its various product categories. It was made clear at the outset that market share would not be traded off for gaining price.

The team proposed meeting the current plan for the coming quarters to be the "goal" regarding revenues, margins, market share, and price levels. The *entitlement value* was to be the sales plan with incremental revenues and margins stemming from a 0.25% increase in average price levels. No one wanted them to be in a state that was worse than that of the preceding 12 months. Therefore, the project team proposed the *baseline* to be the last 12 months of performance in regard to revenues, prices, and margins (see Table 9-1).

Table 9-1   Baseline, Goal, and Entitlement Values of the Six Sigma Pricing Project at Acme in the Define Phase

	Baseline	*Goal*	*Entitlement*
Sales ($$) Total margin ($$) Market share Price	Past 12 months' performance	Same as the plan for current 12 months	Current sales plan plus 0.25% in incremental revenues from price realization with no loss of market share

Charter Item #3: Project Scope

Right at the outset, three main product families within the business unit were chosen to be in the scope of the project. These product families together had a combined annual revenue in the past 12 months of about $400 million, a big percentage of the total revenue for the business division that the general manager headed. Of these revenues, about half were for sales against standing contracts. It was believed that this side of the business would be harder to change, so the focus went to the non-contract half of the business.

The process under consideration was discount management within the quotation process starting with the initial quotation assessment in the field to when the customer was invoiced and the order was shipped (see Figure 9-1).

The project would

- Study the current customer quote process
- Recommend changes to price guidelines as needed
- Develop metrics and report improvements in the price, margin, and market share to track compliance to guidelines
- Recommend corrective actions for noncompliance to modified process

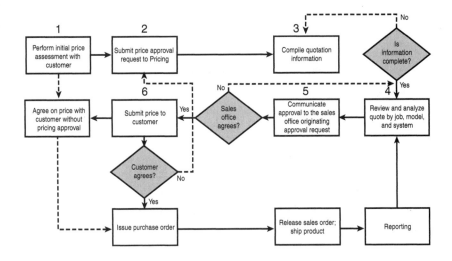

Figure 9-1   High-level process in scope at Acme

Charter Item #4: Resources

The most important resource for this project is the same as any Six Sigma project, the people. Acme had a project team headed by the Pricing manager and a Project Steering Committee headed by the general manager. These two teams had overlapping members to ensure good communication between the project team and the Steering Committee.

The general manager was the project champion and headed the Steering Committee as well. He sat down with the project manager and suggested team members or at least their functional groups for both the Steering Committee and the project team. Based on the functional expertise and leadership support required from various groups, both felt that representation from Marketing, IT, Sales, Finance, and Pricing on both teams would be critical to the success of the project.

The project team comprised

• The general manager of the business unit as *project sponsor*
• The Pricing manager as *project leader*
• The Master Black Belt as *project mentor*
• A Pricing analyst who was expert in accessing the different systems to get price-related data

- The Finance director with many years of experience in the company to validate financial data and to provide insight into pricing numbers
- A product manager who managed the product families that were chosen for this project
- An IT manager to ensure access to data and to validate suggested recommendations from the IT viewpoint.

The Steering Committee included people who were not only stakeholders but individuals with influence and reach within the company. The committee included may of the members of the project team—the project sponsor, the project leader, the project mentor, the product manager, and the Finance director. The committee also included three vice-presidents: (1) the VP of Sales to understand recommendations because the process and any proposed changed would heavily involve Sales reps, (2) the VP of Marketing to make the link between strategy and its implementation at the operational level, and (3) the VP of IT to smooth over any data issues and to understand the implications of any recommendations. Another member was the general manager of another business unit who was interested in carrying out the recommendations at his business unit if the results of the project were positive.

The project leader communicated with the project team that they would communicate as needed, while the Steering Committee would convene for a progress review session for an hour each month. This way, despite the team's size, the time spent on the project would be used efficiently, and the project would not be a serious distraction from doing their "normal" work.

In regard to other resources, the project leader requested only one item, a copy of Minitab software to be installed on his PC at work, for statistical analysis.

Charter Item #5: Expected Benefits

If successful, the Six Sigma project would benefit various customers internal and external to the company. These various "customers" have different "critical-to-quality" attributes or simply said, needs for improvement. *External customers*, that is, the customers of the company, would get clear communication and avoid price-related confusion. From the general manager's viewpoint, margin and sales goals would be met, despite the challenge of the raw material price increase and the company not being sure about the effectiveness or even feasibility of raising list prices. Sales would get quick turnaround on their requests for getting prices/discount approved. Pricing would be able to improve its ability to tighten price bands based on segmentation sales territory, transaction size, and product type. Furthermore, pricing managers and other personnel would be able to remove defects arising from unclear communication, process- and IT-related problems, and incorrectly perceived roles and responsibilities, thus paving the way for continuous improvements in realized price. Of course, all these proposed benefits were constraints on the project team and reflected what project success meant.

Charter Item #6: Project Timeline

The key milestones of the project coincided with the different phases of the project, and the project team scheduled monthly reviews with the Steering Committee accordingly, starting with the presentation at the end of the Define phase to the Steering Committee (see Table 9-2):

Table 9-2   Timeline for the Project at Acme

Phase	Deadline	Report to Steering Committee
Define	Now	Define completed; present to committee
Measure	End of month 1	Measure completed; present to committee
Analyze	End of month 2	Analyze completed; present to committee
Improve; Control	End of month 3	Improve and Control completed; present Final Project Review
Implementation begins	End of month 4	Implementation under way; present preliminary results and future plans

The total project timeline, from start to final presentation (Final Project Review) would require a maximum of 12 weeks plus another four weeks for having enough of the implementation under way to be able to present some results. Although implementation within four weeks seemed aggressive, the assumption was that some of the simple improvements would be made opportunistically even during the Improve and Control phases in month three.

Acme: Differences from a "Typical" Six Sigma Project

Acme's case study for the Define phase shows that any real pricing project done with the Six Sigma approach requires certain compromises. One is that a numerical definition of the problem, as is typical in the Define phase of any Six Sigma project, was not included in the charter. The Pricing manager had estimated the cost of excessive discounts using a sample of invoices and had circulated these numbers around. However, putting the numerical definition of the "problem" in the charter could potentially raise awkward questions. It was easier to pull a number, essentially out of thin air, as entitlement. Given the difficult situation in the market, simply meeting the sales plan was then taken as the goal.

Project duration is of much more significance for pricing projects than it is for other Six Sigma projects. Six Sigma projects typically vary in length from several weeks (Green Belt) to several months (Black Belt). The project at Acme was a Green Belt project, so it had to be reasonably short. However, for pricing projects, shorter projects are generally better than long ones for three reasons: *One*, even small successes can provide a big increase to the bottom line of the division or the company. *Two*, unlike, say manufacturing projects, changes implemented for even successful projects may be rolled back due to various reasons if some of the stakeholders are not happy. If the changes are rolled back, only a small amount of effort would be lost. *Three*, a large project can be an excuse not to do anything. In pricing, there are so many reasons to maintain status quo that a large project with "Six Sigma" or other methodology can become busy work sucking up time and resources in order to avoid or postpone any actions.

Finally, as perhaps in any real project, some of the implementation could precede the final presentation or be carried out soon after. To be true to Six Sigma, a company should begin implementation after the final review of the Six Sigma recommendations (Improve and Control). In reality, many of the project team members and Steering Committee members themselves are able to make small changes to improve the process, so it is simply expedient to do so.

9.7 Summary

The first phase of Six Sigma (and Six Sigma Pricing) is the Define phase. This phase comprises developing the charter, customer requirements, and a high-level process map. Through these three "deliverables," the purpose of this first phase is for the project team to demonstrate that they understand the problem in the context of the process and that they have a realistic scope in mind that can provide attractive benefits.

This chapter described the Define phase at Acme. A real Six Sigma Pricing project requires approval from a diverse group of stakeholders. Therefore, makeup of the project team and the Steering Committee are crucial in ensuring agreement from the Steering Committee to proceed. It is also clear from Acme that there are a number of differences from a typical Six Sigma project for manufacturing or services. The underlying reason for these differences is the number and variety of stakeholders with different interests to protect. These differences capture how Six Sigma Pricing is different from Six Sigma methodology in general.

10

MEASURE PHASE

I never guess. It is a capital mistake to theorize before one has data. Insensibly one begins to twist facts to suit theories, instead of theories to suit facts.

—*Sir Arthur Conan Doyle*

10.1 Introduction

This phase entails two activities: (1) to develop a detailed process map of the "as-is" process and (2) to identify, collect, and present the data we will need for subsequent analysis and design of controls. Recall that in the Define phase we needed data to quantify *the extent of the problem,* that is, the percentage of transactions that were priced too low relative to guidelines. In Measure, the purpose of collecting data is different, being motivated by analysis and design of controls in later phases of the project—Analyze and Control. We shall see later that collecting data for the purpose of control is much more important for pricing projects than it is for manufacturing and service projects.

Analysis and control are connected. We need to collect data for analysis to determine the cause of the undesirable variation in the output (for example, discount level) because if we control the causes of variation, we can also control the proportion of "defects" that are produced as a result. Think of the discount-setting or other pricing process as a machine with control knobs that produces prices or contracts. For different settings of the knobs, we get different values of the output and hence different defect rates. If we can collect data showing different values of the output (Y) with different settings of each input (X), then we can use statistics in the Analyze phase to relate the output to the inputs. With such a relationship, we can suggest controlling the inputs in order to control the output so as to produce fewer defects.

Once we have such a relationship, we can determine how controlling each input will help us control the output of value Y, thus reducing unexplained variation in the output and consequently reducing the number of defects. If one of the X inputs is the transaction size of the entire invoice and we can see from invoice data that, on an average, the discount for any particular SKU increases with the transaction size, we could have pricing guidelines for that SKU that vary with the entire transaction size to better guide the Pricing analysts and Sales personnel.

However, refining guidelines has more to do with control than analysis to understand the root cause of the variation.

Control-driven data collection has a different purpose and is quite pertinent to settings with multiple stakeholders with different interests, as is the case with pricing. We may not always be able to identify the source of the problem, and for pricing, it may be politically incorrect in a corporate setting to discuss how incentives for the different stakeholders contribute to the problem. However, we can still collect data to show the extent of variation in the discount level by customer sales volume, region, product line, and so on and thus be able to produce guidelines that, if enforced well, can decrease the number of transactions for which discounts are "too high" or "too low" compared to those in other transactions.

10.2 Process Map

We have already seen that in the Define phase we make a high-level process map. In Measure, the process map is much more detailed and tries to capture the process as it is followed currently rather than as it was designed. This is particularly relevant for pricing projects because there are many incentives for stakeholders to find shortcuts and workarounds in any process assuming there is a formal process to begin with. There are good reasons for these shortcuts and workarounds depending on one's incentives, but we still need to map the existing process, warts and all. Having team members from different functional areas is beneficial in gaining understanding and being able to communicate the pricing process under consideration.

The purpose of the process map is threefold. The first is simply to capture and convey the reality on the ground, which itself can be quite compelling when we make recommendations. The more data we can gather on the average flows on this process map—for example, number of transactions per day, number of contracts per month, or number of price approvals per day—as well as the variation in terms of measures like range or standard deviation, the better. For instance, a Pricing person may get 50 price approval requests per day, but this may range from as low as 10 to 80 per day. Likewise, the number of requests responded to may range from 40 to 60 per day. As with the Define phase, having a detailed process map shows we have done our homework, but there are other benefits as well.

The second purpose of a process map is analysis. From this viewpoint, the process map provides valuable insight into what data to collect because some subprocesses may be driving a lot of the variation in the output. It is these subprocesses whose outputs we will call as X1, X2, and so on with the output of the overall process being Y. The supplier-inputs-process-outputs-customer (SIPOC) table, mentioned earlier, is helpful in developing the process map and for generating the list of X's for which we need to collect data.

The third purpose of a process map is design of controls. We can collect numbers, even subjective ones, to show the extent people are using workarounds or shortcuts. This can therefore be useful for developing controls or redesigning the process so it is simpler and faster, thus removing some of the need to have shortcuts and workarounds. Data collection on the extent of shortcuts and workarounds will likely be anecdotal and therefore not strictly "Six Sigma" for a purist. However, we have to realize that shortcuts and workarounds exist only because people can cover their tracks and because there is no monitoring built into the process.

As such, the project team has a rather tall order when it comes to mapping the process. Following are some good questions for the team to ask its own members as well as those they interview in mapping the process:

- Who is doing this part of the process?
- What are the "customer" requirements for this part of the process?
- Does this map reflect the current process, or does it represent wishful thinking?
- Where are rework loops?
- What are the non-value-added processes?
- What controls are currently in place?

10.3 Data Collection Plan

Besides mapping out the process—itself a data collection exercise—the team will need to collect data of different types. For pricing projects this may mean collecting invoice or other transaction, bid data, or contract terms. The team should begin planning this data collection using the following four steps:

1. Decide what to measure.
2. Decide on sampling.
3. Agree on operational definitions.
4. Carry out measurement system analysis (MSA).

Step 1: Decide What to Measure

Our choice to measure at the high level will be determined by the extent to which we are going to be analysis-driven or control-driven as discussed earlier. We need to understand what type of analysis we can carry out before collecting data on measures. Eventually, we are trying to control variation in the output measure identified in Define, so our measures should be such that if these are controlled, the output has less variation and therefore fewer defects. It may not be useful to collect data on measures we cannot control, for example, occurrence of hurricanes, because even if we are able to discover that hurricanes cause variation in discount levels, we may not be able do much about their occurrence, at least not directly. In other words, deciding what to measure depends on not only what we can analyze, but also on what we can control in the future to reduce defects.

As we choose what data to collect, we must note the type of data. The type of data is a major pitfall because people unwittingly use incorrect statistical techniques not taking into account the type of data. We need to be aware of the two major types of data, discrete and continuous. The reason is that different statistical techniques apply to the two types of data. Not recognizing the difference between the two data types results in misapplied analysis in the Analyze phase and incorrect recommendations in Improve.

Discrete data is "chunky" because these data pertain typically to categories such as Gender (with values Male/Female), Size (with values Small/Medium/Large), and Management Level (with values Executive/ Manager/Analyst). Sometimes, discrete data take the form of ranks or order (with values First/Second/Third/and so on). Although we can always code these values as numbers, most statistics such as average or standard deviation are not very meaningful. A common error that many people make is to code these categories as numbers, for example, Small/Medium/Large or 1st/2nd/3rd shift as 1/2/3, respectively, and then use statistics as if these were numbers. They are not; they are merely labels. There are statistical techniques that apply to such data: frequency diagrams and frequency counts (how many males and females in the sample data), pie charts, cross-tabs (frequency counts with two variables), and ANOVA, which is discussed in the next chapter.

Continuous data varies smoothly, and the numbers have meaning in themselves—these are not labels for the purpose of categorization. Most of the statistical techniques we are familiar with, such as average, median, correlation, standard deviation, and regression are applicable to this type of data only. An example of continuous data is the discount on a transaction, which can be 34%, 33.2%, or any other rate with any number of decimal places between 0% and 100%. We can meaningfully compute the average discount or the standard deviation. Time, pressure (in psi), conveyor speed (meters/min.), rate (inches/sec.), and cost in euros or dollars are other examples of such data.

Sometimes even when the data is discrete, for example, the number of SKUs purchased by customers in any transaction, we can still consider this data to be continuous for the purpose of statistical analysis. We can consider the number of counted things, for instance, the number of errors in a document or the number of units shipped, as being continuous in most situations for statistical purposes.

Data may be qualitative as well. In some pricing projects, we may find that hard data is difficult to come by because no one captured it in the first instance or because it would be too time-consuming or otherwise awkward to compile. In that case, we may find we have to rely on interviews or focus groups to get qualitative data. Such data is usually categorical (for example, a rating being High/Medium/Low). However, we can also use scales—for instance the so-called Likert 1–7 scale that we can use as continuous data for statistical purposes. Even though there is a propensity to use 1–5 for such things as customer feedback or salesperson feedback, researchers recommend using 1–7, as a wider range captures finer distinctions.

The two types of data are inter-linked in that the same attribute can be measured in either way. However, continuous data can be converted to discrete data but not the other way around. Consider the data on sales by customer for the last fiscal year. These sales numbers are continuous data that we can convert into discrete data. We may choose to devise a new variable called Customer-Type that assigns each customer into one of four categories based on sales: very large, large, medium, or small. Alternatively, we may rank-order customers by their share of the revenue and create a discrete variable called Rank with values 1st, 2nd, 3rd, and so on. Again, from continuous data we can create discrete data, but not the other way around—if all we know is Customer-Type, we cannot figure out Sales or any other continuous data about customers.

Step 2: Decide on Sampling

Sampling is the ultimate pitfall in terms of collecting data, and we can get any results we want (or not) by selecting how we are going to sample. Indeed, most "lying with statistics" is done through clever manipulation of sampling besides old-fashioned misrepresentation with words. Assuming we want to know the "reality" through statistical analysis, we need a truly random sample because statistical analyses apply only to randomly sampled data. This means that if we were going to extract a sample of, say 1,000 invoices from the last 12 months of 200,000 invoices, then each of those 200,000 must have an equal chance of selection for the sample so that there is no "bias" that could affect the results.

In reality, we often use convenience samples whereby data selection for statistical analysis is motivated by convenience. For instance, a colleague may have already spent considerable effort compiling and cleaning up data on invoices from the last two months. It would be convenient to use this data rather than create a random sample from the last 12 months of invoices. When we use convenient samples, we must make an effort to check if there might be a bias in this data that precludes it from representing all invoices from the last 12 months.

Eventually, we are going to be making decisions about the future, so we need to make sure that the data we are using is representative of the future data (that does not obviously exist yet) if the pricing process were to remain the same. If there were changes in the process six months prior, there is no point considering data that is older because it would not represent the future.

The size of the sample is also important. If the sample were too small, even if it were selected without any bias, that is, as a random sample, the small size may itself create a bias because it may not represent the process. It may just be the luck of the draw that the few data points chosen were all too big or all too small and would therefore misrepresent the process we are trying to improve. Therefore, we need to ensure we have a large enough sample size.

Too large of a sample can also be a problem. One reason is the effort required to acquire, clean, and analyze the data. Another reason is that statistically, we can have misleading findings as statistical results that appear to be significant but may actually not be so.

One guideline for generating a sample size is to use 10 to 15 times the number of variables when all these are continuous. When we have discrete data, we may need a lot more because we want 10 to 15 data points for every value of each combination of categories for each variable—for just three discrete variables with four values each, we have 4x4x4=64 combinations! In practice, we may have to make do with less.

Step 3: Agree on Operational Definitions

In pricing, more so than in manufacturing or services, it is important that the different stakeholders agree on what the collected data means. After all, any recommendations we make will be based on this data as facts, and we should not expect stakeholders to buy into our recommendations or agree with each other if they differed in their understanding of what the data represented. Therefore, it is important to have operational definitions on the measures selected and the data collected.

Sometimes we may have a number that we have been given, but such a number is typically from a sample size of one! We should validate such parameters or numbers coming our way. Therefore, we need operational definitions. For instance, someone from Sales may say that they lose 25% of their time waiting for Pricing to respond to them. What does this number mean—complete downtime for Sales personnel or simply a waiting time that they use productively on other matters and therefore not really downtime? Even assuming this number is meaningful, why is it 25%, not 21% or 29%? How was this downtime measured, over what period of time and by whom? Was it a one-time occurrence, or does it happen frequently? Is it an average in the sense that some Sales personnel lose as much as 50% of their productivity and others lose less than 10%, or is it an average in the sense that any particular salesperson loses over 50% of his time in some weeks but less than 10% in other weeks?

Step 4: Carry out Measurement System Analysis (MSA)

Measurement system analysis or MSA is an attempt to avoid another pitfall: assuming that just because we have data especially from computers, it must be correct. In the computer age, and in particular with pricing, there may be a tendency to believe that "we got the data from the system, so it must be right," and no checking is required. Nothing could be farther from the truth. Having more data in computers and the resulting complexity of processes may in fact mean that the proportion of incorrect data is more than it used to be before computers came along.

Pricing-related data are especially vulnerable to inaccuracies that come about as personnel enter numbers as a way to work around the process or around the controls programmed into the system. However good our computer and enterprise systems, people will always be a step ahead in terms of being able to beat restrictions and enter whatever they need to in order to get their jobs done. We are all familiar with grocery store checkout personnel measured for speed scanning one yogurt and entering a count of five when in fact we have bought five different flavors of yogurt. Enterprise systems require much more information for B2B transactions, and there are different motivations for different people entering the data, so the data is even more vulnerable than the yogurt example.

10.4 Acme

After the senior management ratified the charter for a Green Belt project, the project team carried out the steps required in the Measure phase of the project with guidance from the Black Belt mentor.

Process Map

The project leader used the supplier-input-process-output-customer (SIPOC) approach described in Chapter 7, "Tools for Six Sigma," (see section, "Tools for Measure") to develop a detailed as-is process map. The intention of this process map was to identify all value-added and non-value-added process steps, inputs (X's) in each process, and the resulting outputs (Y's).

Different members of the team interviewed Sales, IT, Pricing, and Finance people. They followed the first input from the customer and how it flowed through the company's personnel, systems, and processes leading back to the customer as final output. During the interviews, the project team documented sources of information and collected samples of data, identifying systems and the people and processes that used them. They also marked each process input uncontrollable (U) or controllable (C) depending on if it was in or out of process control (that is, processes that were controlled or could be influenced by Pricing relatively easily). The SIPOC table reflected leaks and inefficiencies in the process even before any formal analysis had begun. These were marked for immediate attention rather than left to wait until the end of project for implementation.

The project team discovered a number of small problems while developing the process map. These problems were small enough for the project team and others to fix even as the project progressed. From a purist perspective, all fixes should come later. However, when fixes are easy and noncontroversial, the project team members who are also involved with the process in their normal jobs will find it tempting to do so as the problems are uncovered.

1. **Price assessment with customer**: Many experienced sales-people knew the larger customers in their sales territories and were pricing all customers based on experience rather than checking with Pricing for correct price. They would easily commit to a lower price and simply inform Pricing of their decision rather than seek approval. Then there was the case of less experienced Sales reps, or sometimes experienced ones, who offered such high prices that the customer just walked away.

2. **Quotation request**: Salespeople were required to submit quotation requests using a specified format with an expected turn-around within one business day. Pricing people would waste time in following up when such critical information as competitive price to justify a lower price was missing. This process was out of control and required correction.

3. **Quotation request**: The project team also found that the quotation requests from a given sales territory were mapped to a specific pricing analyst. If the analyst went on vacation or sick leave, the requests would just remain in the queue. There could be an easy fix to bring this step in control.

4. **Compiling information for quotation**: The information needed for a single quote resided in three order-entry systems, two of which did not talk to each other. The pricing analysts required time to manually type data in the quotation system, increasing chances of manual error and adding 15–20 person-hours of non-value-added work weekly.

5. **Review of quotation request**: The examination of the process revealed that prices were set based on national benchmarks that did not discriminate by sales territory, transaction size, or seasonality. The competitive information provided was fictional—always 3 to 5% lower than the requested price. This way the Sales reps could emphasize how hard they had negotiated, and that they were always winning the customer's confidence and retained price leadership in the market. Pricing analysts had little basic knowledge, if any, on the product value. They were required to communicate with product managers for large transactions or custom products but occasionally took the shortcut and priced by gut feel.

6. **Communication with Sales office**: Salespeople were extremely sensitive when Pricing rejected their price approval requests without any suggestion for an alternate price point. Fixing this problem would reduce frustration incurred in the process.

7. **Quotation to invoice**: This step revealed that many Sales reps requested extremely low prices but offered much higher prices to customers. While this helped the Sales rep in increasing their commission, the process also introduced variation in pricing.

8. **Reporting and tracking**: There was a large amount of price-related reporting that was of limited practical use. There were at least three problems: First, many of the reports had inconsistent information because they used different databases not connected to each other. Second, there were over 200 active reports, but no one knew who the owners were for more than 150 of these! Yet, dedicated IT personnel and systems developed these reports regularly and in many cases shipped them nationwide. Finally, useful information like the hit rate—ratio of orders to approved discounts for any calendar month—could not be tracked at all.

Measurement Systems Analysis

It was quite important to ensure the measurement systems were accurate and to check whether IT systems or humans involved in the discount approval were contributing to the variation in the measurement. Process mapping had revealed manual input of data twice on the quotation process since two of the three systems were not linked electronically. The project manager took the results from the SIPOC table as a starting point and checked the databases themselves as well as the manual data entry into one of these databases.

The Six Sigma mentor often reminded the team members, "Do not trust that the data from the computers are always correct." The team did not really understand this point until they delved into data with the help of a capable Pricing analyst. They worked with two different databases: the invoice database and the quotation database.

The team downloaded detailed invoice-level order data for the previous 24 months from the invoice database and started looking for completeness of information. Despite hundreds of thousands of records of data in their database, simple conditional queries in Microsoft Access revealed useful information:

- **Missing records**: Data older than one year did not have over one-fourth of the records. After checking with Finance and IT, the team found that the company systematically archived all records 365 days after the payments were received or the product returned. This meant that many records older than a year may just have been archived in a different database that was difficult to access. The team therefore decided to use only the data of the most recent year for analysis.
- **Missing list prices**: A tiny fraction, 39 records out of almost 400,000, had missing list prices. After locating the source of the error to a one-time glitch, the team excluded these erroneous records from analysis.
- **Missing cost information**: Over a quarter (26%) of the records were missing cost information. However, this highlighted a huge problem—Pricing personnel did not know cost numbers when approving discount requests, though they were expected to use margin thresholds when approving discounts. The missing data would have caused greater worry if these numbers were being used for financial reporting. Fortunately, the team discovered that Finance used only high-level cost and revenue data to calculate gross margin as opposed to a roll-up of transactional figures.
- **Missing part numbers**: About one-tenth of the records were missing part numbers. The team was able to quickly repair these records with help from IT. The team also informed IT and asked them to find and correct the problem, which they did by finding a bug in the system and fixing it within the same week.
- **Missing discount codes**: A small number of records (less than one in 200) were missing discount codes despite a specific discount having been used in the transaction. The number of records was small

enough that these could be dropped from the dataset being used for analysis. However, IT logged this as a system problem that required fixing.

The team's review of the quotation database also brought up a few problems:

- **Missing discount codes:** In a small number of records, the pricing analysts had forgotten to input the appropriate discount code.
- **Erroneous representation of discount code:** In a large number of cases (over 30%), there were problems with how the discount code was represented. For instance, the analysts were required to follow a certain convention that included a hyphen. In many cases, the analysts had forgotten to include the hyphen or had placed it incorrectly. The project manager sought help from IT to fix his sample data and asked for simple programming support to alleviate problems of this nature.

Next, the team looked into the accuracy of manual data entry into the quotation database. The project manager realized this part of the MSA would be a manual check and that he would need to check data entry errors by all the five analysts responsible for responding to price approval requests by Sales personnel. For each analyst, he sampled 10 approvals that had come via fax and compared the information in the fax with what the analysts had entered in the quotation database. In all cases, the data were 100% consistent between the information on the faxed request and the corresponding entries in the quotation database record. Assuming this accuracy held across other records as well, manual data entry by pricing analysts could be eliminated as a source of measurement error.

The data the team needed pertained to invoices as well as quotations, but these resided in different databases. To get consistent data from these two databases, the project manager first compared the information fields available in them. Indeed, there were fields of interest to the team that were available only in the quotation database (see Table 10-1).

Table 10-1   Data Fields in the Invoice and Quotations Databases—entries marked (*) were deemed useful for data analysis

Quotation Database	Invoice Database
Discount code (along with discount type)	Discount code (along with discount type)*
N/A	Transaction code*
Price approved by Pricing*	Price offered by Sales to Customer*
Geography—Market, Territory, Pricing Analyst	Geography—Market, Territory*
Date, Month, Quarter, Year	Date, Month, Quarter, Year*
Product—Bill of Materials available	Product—Bill of Materials available*
N/A	Price approver by name*
Transaction Size	Transaction Size*
Cost*	Cost—not reliable
N/A	Sales Commission amount
Competitor information (not reliable)	N/A
Status—Won/pending/lost (not reliable)	Status (implicit)—Won only

Given the differences between quoted (approved) and invoiced prices, the project manager requested that a single MS Access database be made with records downloadable from both databases. This was a small project for one programmer but had a big payoff not only for the project team but also for the Pricing team in general. The team could then download linked data for the last 12 months from both databases and go on to data analysis in the next phase.

10.5 Summary

The Measure phase entails (1) developing a detailed process map of the "as-is" process and (2) identifying, collecting, and presenting the data needed for subsequent analysis and design of controls. In developing a process map using a tool like SIPOC (see Chapter 7), it is good to ask questions about whether the map reflects the current process or something that is merely desired. We need to pay particular attention to rework loops and existing controls. At Acme, developing the process map resulted in identifying many problems and sources of friction between Sales and Pricing that could be fixed as the work proceeded.

Before collecting data, the team should plan this effort using the following four steps: decide what to measure; decide on sampling; agree on operational definitions; and carry out a measurement system analysis (MSA). The last one is important because pricing-related or transaction information in computers are especially vulnerable to inaccuracies resulting from personnel entering numbers to work around the process or around the controls programmed into the system. At Acme, the project team discovered a number of errors in the quotations and the invoice databases as they sought to extract a sample of transactions for data analysis.

11

ANALYZE PHASE

*I think we ought always to entertain our opinions
with some measure of doubt. I shouldn't wish people
dogmatically to believe any philosophy, not even mine.*

—Bertrand Russell (1872–1970)

11.1 Introduction

Analysis is the heart of Six Sigma, as it is for any quality approach. The purpose of the *Analyze* phase is to identify and understand the reasons for the variation of the output measure and/or ways that this variation can be controlled. Statistics is useful for this analysis but is only a part of this, because there are other ways of identifying reasons for defects.

Suppose the output measure is the discount for a flagship SKU in transactions. The variation in discounts results in some transactions having too high (or too low) of a discount level, resulting in not only the company losing money (or customers' trust) now but also in future transactions with the same customer by setting their expectations. We may want to know why discount levels vary so much. Alternatively, we may only want to know how to control the discount levels in future transactions if we do not want to address the "why" explicitly.

There are three types of analyses, all pertaining to the process we want to improve: (1) process analysis to understand process failures that lead to a defective output, (2) root-cause analysis to hypothesize reasons for defects and validate a plausible subset, and (3) data analysis to link the variation in the output measure to some of the inputs.[1] All three analyses are closely related because we use them on the same process to discover what is causing the variation in the output measure, for instance, discount level or contract terms. Whether we use all three in all situations depends on the objectives and what is technically or politically feasible.

There are two important points about these three analyses. First, while data analysis is statistically driven, it does not mean we have to be statisticians to carry out such analysis. We can use a spreadsheet to produce simple graphs like scatter-plots (X-Y charts) or cross-tabulation counts to get a good start—such simple analysis may even be adequate. Second, process analysis and root-cause analysis are not statistics-driven, so we can do a Six Sigma project, even a Six Sigma Pricing project with lots of data, without doing "statistics." Moreover, much of business school training in statistics can lead to the misapplication of statistical techniques because such training typically focuses on continuous data, whereas much of the data we would be analyzing is likely discrete.

There is also the question of order in which we should do the three analyses if we are doing all three. The first should always be process analysis, especially for pricing-related projects because different stakeholders may have a different understanding of what the process is as well as what it could or should be. Only after doing process analysis should we attempt root-cause analysis or data analysis. Statistics is perceived to be paramount importance in any quality initiative—one reason Lean Manufacturing is so popular is that it does not involve statistics—so there may be pressure to start with data analysis and generate professional-looking graphs and statistics, but the other two analyses help understand what is important and which statistical analyses might be useful.

11.2 Process Analysis

The process we are trying to improve may be quite complicated, so one purpose of *process analysis* is to narrow the focus on certain subprocesses or steps, and another is to specify the process as it occurs in the current situation based on interviews. It is also possible that the process is simply unspecified or undocumented, which is quite likely in a pricing-related setting, so another purpose of process analysis is to show how all the process steps contribute to the problem. Process analysis results in questions whose answers we can seek through root-cause or data analyses.

Thus there are two main purposes of process analysis: one, to understand the reasons behind variation or defects in the context of process by considering its various steps and two, to list questions whose answers will help us improve the process. Other approaches besides Six Sigma attempt to achieve the same objectives, and we should feel comfortable using these. For instance, if the organization uses the Lean approach or some other process improvement methodology, we can use it along with the vocabulary that goes with the process analysis carried out with this methodology.

We need to look at the process broken down into detailed subprocesses and steps in the Measure phase along with most, if not all, variants that take place in reality. For pricing-related processes, we should expect variants and alternative steps that have taken place in the past. These variants—shortcuts or workarounds—may happen for good reasons, but nonstandard processes invariably lead to variation in contract terms or discount levels.

Process analysis should lead us to ask questions, to be answered with root-cause and data analyses, about the variants in the process—and about failures. Questions could include the following:

- Why does it take more than 24 hours to process a pricing approval request for a customer who has purchased the same product many times before at the same discount level?
- Why does a salesperson sometimes offer a price to a customer below the pre-authorized level without seeking price approval? Does this apply only to new customers or also to existing customers?

There are many tools for process analysis because business processes lie at the heart of any organization. We should use any approach that our organization is already using. Three tools typically used in Six Sigma projects are as follows—we discussed these tools for process analysis in detail in Chapter 7, "Tools for Six Sigma":

- Cause-and-effect (C&E) matrix is a systematic way to quantify the impact of each step in the current process on customer requirements and hence the extent of causing "defects."
- Failure Mode Effect Analysis (FMEA) is a way to understand how processes can "fail" in the sense of producing defective output. FMEA helps prioritize which issues to fix with a multifunctional team rating problems on how severe impact of an occurrence is ("severity"), how often it occurs ("occurrence"), and how easy it is to detect in real time ("detectability").
- Value-stream analysis comes from Lean Manufacturing, and focuses on identifying the steps that add value and those that do not with a goal to eliminate unnecessary steps and other waste. For pricing

processes, the transformation applies to information in the form of status—a proposed price turns into an approved price that in turn changes into an invoiced price. Value-stream analysis could be quite useful in understanding and reducing the time it takes for Pricing to respond to salespersons' requests for price approvals.

11.3 Root-Cause Analysis

Root-cause analysis attempts to answer the questions that have come up in process analysis, and in doing so, get to the underlying cause of the defects or failures in the process. However, its real value lies in getting a variety of people to buy into the underlying causes and understand the reason for targeting these causes.

As such, root-cause analysis is always a group exercise that involves brainstorming to (1) identify possible explanations, (2) narrow down the possibilities through consensus, and (3) validate or at least agree on the underlying causes to target. As with any brainstorming exercise, we can think of this type of analysis as diverging into a large number of possible explanations and then converging onto to a much smaller set of explanations that are more likely than the ones dropped.[2]

It is important that these diverge-converge steps in any brainstorming session are kept separate. One way is to document all possible explanations generated by the group. A check is also needed on group members attempting to eliminate possible explanations put forth by others during the diverge step.

Of course, brainstorming is vulnerable to the same group dynamics that come to fore in any group situation. For instance, the louder or more politically skilled group members can steer the discussion toward their pet peeves that may have little to do with the problem at hand. This is why some people prefer using written ideas on cards or sticky notes to verbal discussion. Either way, in the hands of a skillful facilitator, root-cause analysis can lead to consensus building that can greatly ease subsequent implementation of the recommendations coming out of the project.

In regard to tools—again, refer to Chapter 7 for details—a fishbone diagram is quite useful in generating possible explanations, visually communicating these, and then dropping or organizing these in two or more levels of causes. We can also use categories of causes like Machine, Methods, Measurement, Nature, People, and Materials, or stakeholder functions as categories.

As we discussed before in Chapter 7, there are three ways to identify root causes: First, find out if any first or second-level cause occurs in multiple places; second, collect data on which cause is associated more frequently with the effect; and third, use voting or multivoting within the team (or a focus group) whereby the team members vote as many causes "in" as they want, and the ones at the high end become the focus of discussion.

11.4 Data Analysis

The purpose of data analysis is to try to understand an output measure's possible relationship with other input measures. These possible relationships are an attempt to seek answers to some of the questions that resulted from process analysis done earlier. With Six Sigma being a quality-driven approach, many may think that this step is critical to any Six Sigma project. Indeed, it is quite useful in the fact-and-data-based reasoning that distinguishes Six Sigma from many other process improvement approaches.

Typically, we may seek to employ statistics to link the values of the output measure, denoted by Y, to various input measures termed the X's that are related to the subprocess inputs or are attributes. For instance, if the output measure is discount level (Y) in any transaction, then the size of the transaction (X1), the region for delivery (X2), and size of the customer's purchases in the past 12 months (X3) may all be attributes that we may seek to link with the discount level. If the total time for price approval (Y) is the output measure, then the number of times a request goes back and forth due to incomplete information may be one of the process inputs (X).

For data analysis to be meaningful, we must know two things: First, we must know whether the data are continuous or discrete so that we can apply the right techniques, not just the ones we happen to know. As mentioned earlier, this is a major pitfall in data analysis with the responsibility partly lying with business school education. Second, we must know what we are trying to find out, at least what we are trying to link to which measure to which other measure(s).

As discussed in Chapter 7, a simple guide to the choice of techniques is as follows. When the output Y is continuous, use ANOVA if the inputs are discrete categories. For instance, we can use ANOVA to test whether different sales regions have the same average discounts.

When the output Y is continuous (that is, discount level as a percentage), use scatter plots, correlation, and multiple regression if all the inputs X1, X2, X3, and so on are continuous. Scatter plots reveal indicative patterns if any between these inputs and the output although a pattern, whether cigar-shaped or other, does not indicate we have found a root cause. If we get cigar-shaped patterns, then and only then can we use some other statistics like correlation analysis and regression analysis. Recall that regression analysis is the statistical equivalent of drawing a straight line through the points and listing the parameters of this straight line, called regression coefficients.

When the data comprises ranks for both output Y and input X, you can use rank-order correlation to indicate whether the two ranks are linked with each other positively or negatively. Even when data are continuous, rank-order correlations can be quite useful because the computations do not get distorted by extreme values or by how the data are distributed.

When the output Y is discrete, we use cross-tabulation (and the associated chi-square statistics) when the inputs are discrete. We use logit regression when the inputs are continuous. Logit regression is quite useful to understand how discount levels are related to bids being won or lost.[3]

11.5 Acme

The project team gained insight in the data capabilities, system efficiencies, measuring tools, and people during the Measure phase as discussed in the previous chapter. The Analyze phase was a smooth continuation with process analysis, root-cause analysis, and data analysis.

Process Analysis—C&E Matrix and FMEA

The team used the cause-and-effect or C&E matrix for process analysis. While mapping the process itself in the Measure phase, the project leader and the Six Sigma mentor observed that most issues were process-related and could be fixed in two to three months. The team then did a C&E matrix analysis. The analysis revealed that the top problem listed was the Sales reps' proposal and communication of the price to the customer at the very beginning of the process.

Next, the team did FMEA even though it initially seemed unnecessary after the C&E analysis. However, when the project team scored the initial setting and communicating of price by Sales rep, they discovered the issue scored high on Occurrence and Severity but extremely low on Detectability, that is, the ability of existing controls to detect the problem. This made the multiple of the three scores, or the Risk Priority Number, quite low. There was no data or independent witness to point to the salesperson not having properly managed the initial contact with the customer. Hence, the incorrect price initially offered by the Sales rep became a low priority. In fact, the team excluded it from the scope of the project and put it on the parking lot for Sales to handle in future negotiation workshops.

The use of C&E and FMEA tools initially seemed pointless or "busy-work" for the project team as well as for the Steering Committee. The fact that the project was Green Belt added to the perception that use of such tools was simply part of the Six Sigma "bureaucracy."

However, the resulting consensus to fix things that had festered for years in the pricing processes belied this initial misperception. The use of FMEA after a fairly straightforward C&E analysis also prevented the derailment of the project.

Root-cause Analysis

The project team then did *root-cause analysis* on the variation in discount levels across transactions. Process analysis had already pointed to variations in practices between different Sales offices and regions. Therefore, the team focused the root-cause analysis effort on these issues. One result was the confirmation that regions and Sales offices were root causes in the variation, although the team did not explore reasons why this was the case. The discussions made it clear that data analysis could help confirm this statistically. If indeed this were the case, Pricing could use the results of the data analysis to help create different guidelines for different regions.

Data Analysis

The measurement systems analysis, or MSA, in the previous phases resulted in the team choosing only the last 12 months' data from the 24 months' data that were available. Recall that the team pulled in linked data from the quotation and invoice databases to explain different X's that caused variation in *price level*, which is the invoiced price as a fraction of list price, that is, *price level = 1 - discount level*. The project team used statistics for testing validity of long-standing beliefs in the company regarding the price level.

The team added a field, Region, to the linked data collected in Measure. This field depicted the sales territory for each transaction and had five corresponding values: Central (C), Northeast (NE), South (S), Southeast (SE), and West (W). Another discrete grouping applied to the data was the "Quarter" in the calendar year with possible values "1st," "2nd," "3rd," and "4th," depending on the invoice date.

Although transaction size (total sales) for the invoice is a continuous number, the team created discrete categories for this variable so that all the input or X variables would be discrete. For instance, they grouped data by "Transaction Size" depending on total sales in an invoice, namely, "$5K" (for $0 to 5000), "$10K" (for invoice amounts from 5000+ to 10,000), and so on, up to individual large transactions of up to $200,000. This categorization would also be helpful in creating new discount guidelines based on the size of the transaction.

UNDERSTAND VARIATION IN PRICE LEVELS

The project leader started with a simple histogram to study the variation in price levels and found it to be quite large (see Figure 11-1). The project leader then proceeded to study relationships between price levels as the output Y with transaction size, region, and seasonality as input variables X.

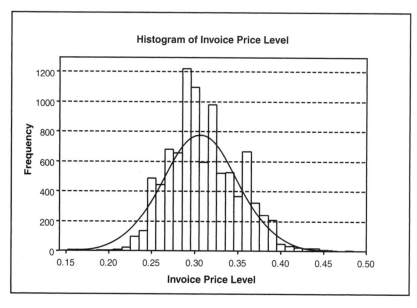

Figure 11-1   The variation in price level at Acme

VARIABILITY IN PRICE LEVELS BY DIFFERENT TRANSACTION SIZE

The effect of transaction size was always a topic of heated debate between Pricing and Sales. At Acme, Sales personnel insisted that the customers did not want to pay more (as a percentage of list price) for a small transaction than they did for a large transaction (recall these are not customers on a price contract, and many purchases were one-off transactions). However, they asked for deeper discounts when a large transaction was being negotiated, and these deep discounts could then become a basis for discounts for small transactions as well. This made Pricing reluctant to approve requested discounts on large transactions as well, requiring a senior manager to step in to approve discounts for large transactions.

One serendipitous outcome of this analysis was the discovery that there were many quotation requests for small transactions where special discounts were generally not required. Still, these requests took time for analysts to approve, and Sales personnel had to wait unduly long even for these requests. This indicated there was an opportunity to streamline the process by giving more flexibility to the Sales offices to negotiate the price with the customer without seeking approval from Pricing.

Data analysis in the form of a boxplot of price levels at different transaction sizes showed that the larger transactions had lower price levels (that is, higher discounts) on average. The range also tended downward for pricing levels as the transaction size increased (see Figure 11-2).

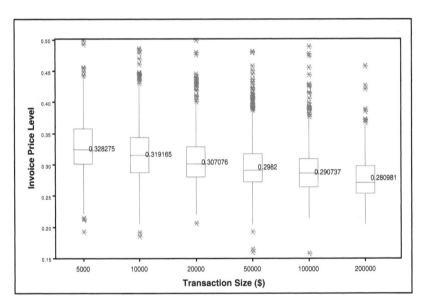

Figure 11-2   Boxplot of price levels at different transaction sizes

Still, there was a large variation in invoiced price levels in all markets for every product family in all transaction sizes. A histogram for price levels at different transaction sizes showed the overlap in price levels. This suggested that although on average smaller transactions had higher price levels (smaller discounts), there were many transactions for which the discounts were too low or too high relative to the average level for that transaction size.

For many transactions, large or small, the corresponding discounts did not fit the overall pattern of larger discounts for larger orders. This meant the company was losing profits directly when the discounts were too large on individual transactions relative to the overall pattern. The company was likely losing money even when the discounts were too small for the transaction size relative to the overall pattern because the customer would eventually find out that the price was too high and either stop buying in the future or negotiate harder in future transactions (see Figure 11-3).

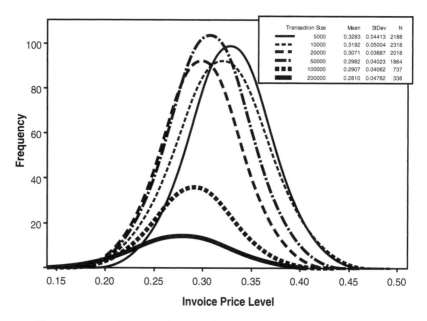

Transaction Size	Mean	StDev	N
5000	0.3283	0.04413	2188
10000	0.3192	0.05004	2318
20000	0.3071	0.03887	2018
50000	0.2982	0.04023	1864
100000	0.2907	0.04062	737
200000	0.2810	0.04782	338

Figure 11-3   Histogram for price levels at different transaction sizes

Comparing approved prices and the prices that were eventually invoiced proved interesting. A histogram for price levels approved by Pricing (based on Sales personnel requests) and price levels invoiced to the customer showed that for all transaction sizes, Sales reps requested prices lower than what they eventually got from the customer (see Figure 11-4). On an average, the approved prices were significantly lower (5–8%) than prices actually paid by customers. Seasoned members of the project team suggested that the reps pushed harder on the internal price negotiation with Pricing to give themselves more room for negotiation with the customer.

There may have been a second reason as well. The company had a two-tier sales commission structure with a higher commission for any amount invoiced above the approved price, effectively giving an incentive to Sales personnel to negotiate with Pricing analysts to lower the approved price and then increase the invoiced price charged to the customers. The company, therefore, lost profits when the approved price was low even if the Sales rep got a much higher invoiced price because of excessive sales commissions.

There were many transactions where the reverse held true, for instance, the invoiced price was lower than the approved price (as discussed in Chapter 9, "Define Phase"). Some Sales reps had figured out how to use old discount codes that should have expired as well as ways to keep them active in the quotation system. This was an important leak to fix.

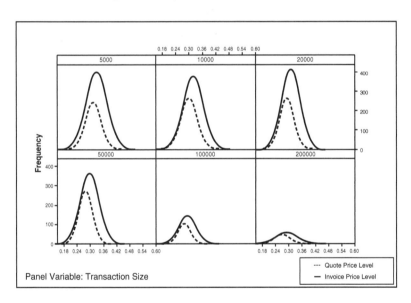

Figure 11-4   Histogram (with normal approximation) with approved price levels and invoiced price levels by different transaction sizes

Further analysis by region showed that the differential between quoted and invoiced price levels varied significantly across regions. This pattern was even more visible for different transaction sizes. Some regions invoiced at price levels fairly close to the quoted prices, while others showed large differences. The project leader probed further and found that regions with large differences had much higher sales commissions even when the sales volume was the same as other regions. This was further indication that the two-tier sales commission structure was encouraging some personnel to not only push up invoiced prices as much as they could with customers but also bargain down the approved price.

PRICE LEVELS IN DIFFERENT QUARTERS

Histograms showed price-level variation in different seasons. They showed that the product was seasonal with both sales and average invoiced price levels being higher in the spring and the summer quarters than in the other two quarters. Historically, guidelines for price levels had been set to be the same throughout the year, yet in peak selling season the requested prices went up drastically. This meant the company would do well to develop season pricing.

COMPETITIVE ANALYSIS

Although the MSA had ruled out competitive data as being unreliable, the project leader checked variation in price level for different competitors. The data showed that the quotations in the sample data referred to the same one or two of the largest competitors. The team could not pursue analysis by competitor but made a note to mention this fact to the project Steering Committee.

ADVANCED STATISTICAL ANALYSIS

The project team used ANOVA, one of the statistical tools, for hypothesis testing. There were several hypotheses held by the Sales and Pricing people in the company. Capturing and documenting key beliefs held by people in Sales, Pricing, Marketing, and other functions was easy because of the many years of history of discord based on these beliefs.

The project team devised statistical tests along the lines of the preceding analyses on price levels. They first stated the default or "null" hypothesis (H_0) and an alternative hypothesis (H_a) for different analyses. If the test rejected the null hypothesis with high confidence, the project team would accept the alternative hypothesis as being "true." If however the test failed to reject the null hypothesis, the team would live with that as being "true" at least from a work viewpoint using "innocent until proven guilty" logic.

The first test was to check if price levels in all transaction sizes were the same. The project manager set the hypothesis as follows:

Null hypothesis H_0= Invoiced price level is the same for all transaction sizes

Alternative hypothesis H_a = Not the same across all transaction sizes

The one-way ANOVA test (Figure 11-5) showed that the team could easily reject the null hypothesis with a confidence of almost 100% (100% minus the probability value that turned out to be zero up to three decimal places). It was clear that variation in discounts was linked to transaction size. The implication, then, was that the company could control this variation relative to guideline price levels, by ensuring that the guidelines on price levels were based on transaction size.

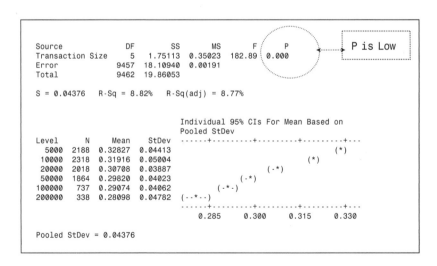

Figure 11-5   Results of ANOVA test for invoiced price levels
by transaction size

The second analysis was to test whether the price levels were the same in all Sales regions—something the company believed and therefore had one set of price guidelines for the entire country. Again, the ANOVA showed that this null hypothesis could be rejected with a high degree of confidence. This meant that the region was a factor in causing variations in price levels. To counter this variation, guideline price levels would have to be developed by region.

The third analysis was to test whether price levels in all seasons were the same because many in the company believed that the business was not seasonal. Here too, the ANOVA results clearly showed that this null hypothesis could be rejected and that seasonality was a factor behind price level variation. This called for price guidelines to be developed by season.

The ANOVA tests confirm what is visually available from the histograms. While statistical analysis is invaluable, lack of confidence in statistics availability should not deter anyone from pursuing a Six Sigma Pricing project especially as spreadsheets and easy-to-use statistical packages have many graphical tools.

11.6 Summary

Having done process mapping and data collection in the Measure phase, the team can carry out three types of analyses in the Analyze phase. These are (1) *process analysis* to understand process failures that lead to a defective output, (2) *root-cause analysis* to hypothesize reasons for defectives and validating a plausible subset, and (3) *data analysis* to quantify the link between the output measure and some of the inputs. Not all projects will require all three. Statistics is useful for data analysis only, and even that may be something requiring only simple tools such as scatter plots, histograms, box-plot charts, and cross-tabulation.

The project team at Acme used C&E matrix and FMEA for process analysis. Both seemed to be overkill initially but turned out to be quite useful eventually in creating the consensus and the collective will to carry out changes. Root-cause analysis was rudimentary but helped prepare the ground for data analysis by focusing the team's attention on some potential causes of variation in discount levels.

For data analysis, the team used discount level as the continuous output variable Y and region, quarter, and invoice transaction size as input variables X. They found that the discount levels varied by all of these input variables, both visually (using box plot charts) and statistically using ANOVA. Therefore, data analysis showed that pricing guidelines had to be different for different regions, quarters, and transaction sizes. This information, while not providing "underlying causes" of price variations, would be the basis of designing new controls.

12

IMPROVE AND CONTROL PHASES

We improve ourselves by victories over ourself.

—Edward Gibbon (1737–1794)

12.1 Introduction

During the Analyze phase, it should be clear to the project team which solutions it can recommend to control variation in the output of the process in question or otherwise improve its effectiveness. However, we need a formal process of listing and prioritizing solutions before presenting to the Steering Committee. This is the purpose of the Improve phase.

For a typical Six Sigma project, the project team identifies possible improvements and prioritizes these for presentation to the Steering Committee. The Improve phase is followed by the Control phase during which the team designs controls to ensure improvements are implemented and achieved.

For Six Sigma Pricing projects, however, improvements will likely take the form of controls when it comes to improving realized prices. Improvements for projects like decreasing the turnaround time for price approval requests may not take the form of traditional controls. However, given the multiple functions involved, most projects will need controls for improvement. Therefore, Improve and Control phases for Six Sigma Projects go hand in hand and we discuss both these phases in this chapter.

With the Six Sigma Pricing project ending after the Improve and Control phases, we also need to create a hand-off document that has the "to-be" process with solutions and process controls built into it.

12.2 Improve

During Analyze, the project team identified and estimated the impact of different sources of variation. The next step is to create a proposal that takes the analysis to a potential solution to bridge the gap between baseline value and the project target. In doing so, the members from different functions on the project team should understand the risks. It is imperative for them to suggest tracking mechanisms to identify improvement over baseline and thus "close the loop" after the solutions have been implemented.

To prioritize proposed solutions, one tool is the prioritization matrix, similar to the C&E matrix, for a group exercise to build consensus and a shared understanding among the team members from different functions. A simpler version is the payoff matrix with business impact on the vertical axis and ease of implementation or effort on the horizontal axis. We discussed these tools in Chapter 7, "Tools for Six Sigma."

To identify and communicate the risks associated with implementation, the project team can use FMEA. In the Improve phase, the team uses FMEA to convey to the Steering Committee how the implementation of the proposed solutions can fail rather than how the process fails, as we saw before in the Analyze phase. FMEA thus provides a way to convey the risks in a comprehensive and apolitical manner.

12.3 Control

There are two reasons for designing controls: (1) to check if the approved recommendations are actually being carried out and (2) to check if the results being sought in terms of process improvement are actually being achieved. Eventually, controls are very much a part of the modified process to ensure that it is standardized, that is, to ensure that the process takes place as expected and therefore results in far fewer defects than before.

Implementing the solutions can be quite tricky even after receiving approval from the Steering Committee. Therefore, controls on the implementation, even if these are simple progress reports, can be quite useful. This is especially true if the audience for these reports comprises senior managers who have agreed to the implementation via the Steering Committee.

However, the project team should strive to ensure that the proposed controls are not onerous. This is because even after implementation and the desired improvement is documented after implementation, making the modifications to the process stick is tricky. Pricing projects are not like manufacturing or services projects where there is a clear win-win situation for all stakeholders concerned. Not all stakeholders for pricing projects may perceive themselves as coming out ahead with the improvements to the process, regardless of the impact to the bottom line of the company. The tendency after initial success may be to unravel or dilute the controls using the argument that the controls have now been "internalized" and are therefore not needed any more. The best thing to counter such arguments is to design controls that do not get in the way of people doing their work as before but still ensure that management will be informed the frequency of any infringements.

We discussed control charts, exception codes, and scorecards in Chapter 7 as tools to achieve control. Control charts will typically have upper and lower control limits, but they can be used without limits to indicate *trends* and *shifts* in price levels or other measures. Exception codes are quite useful for controlling workarounds and shortcuts without imposing strict process controls that do not allow any flexibility in the process. If senior management is tracking exceptions and is known to be doing so regularly, then exceptions reporting can be a powerful tool for achieving control without extensive change management. Scorecards present a limited number of carefully chosen measures that together describe the overall state of the process in question or of pricing in general.

12.4 Final Presentation

The final presentation summarizes the objectives, issues, as well as resolutions and metrics that delineate the accomplishments of the overall project. It covers the Define, Measure, Analyze, Improve, and Control (DMAIC) phases to show any surprises encountered during the project, what steps worked exceedingly well, and which steps although essential may not be needed in a Six Sigma Pricing project. Keep in mind that the presentation is really about the recommendations (and preliminary or estimated benefits) as well as future steps.

The project summary should underscore the roles and responsibilities as well as the follow up process involving the Steering Committee. Most likely, the same project team or at least the project manager will be charged with implementation under the same committee. Lastly, although not a Six Sigma mandate, the project leader should acknowledge the support and contribution of the team members and others in the company.

12.5 Acme

The project team had found several opportunities for improvement while navigating through the Define, Measure, and Analyze phases of the project. Some of the problems were fixed easily after informal consultation with Steering Committee members even before the conclusion of the project, while others required going through the Improve and Control phases.

The project team devised improvement actions for most issues that had come up in Analyze. Some issues such as the linking of the quotation and invoice databases did not require a control plan and were implemented straightaway. Other actions related to making behavioral changes presented a challenge. Six Sigma projects in manufacturing settings deal with measurement specifications, but how do we influence human behavior for positive change? The Improve plan had to do better than just provide a mechanical solution for issues that had remained unresolved for years.

The project leader, the project sponsor, and the general manager of the business in which the chosen products were in scope discussed the company culture and agreed that the idea of "controlling" Sales personnel from negotiating freely with customers would be viewed negatively. They also discussed preemptive and detective controls for the pricing problems at Acme. Preemptive controls would be those that would block any potential problem (defect) before happening, for example, a salesperson asking for a low price due to competitive reasons would get a flat refusal based on the stated guidelines. Detective controls would allow a discount higher than that allowed by guidelines but would track and report problems or potential problems.

As an example of a preemptive control, the price quotation system was programmed not to allow a lower price level unless validated by an exception code showing approval from a pricing manager or a member of the leadership team. Detective controls were deemed appropriate where there was low detectability, for instance, if a salesperson was coerced by an unusually aggressive customer to agree to a low price or forever lose business. In such cases, a review of the monthly exception code report would show the frequency of these instances—if this frequency related to a small set of Sales reps or to a certain sales territory. Based on such reasoning, the project team started developing new processes and reports to instill behavior change.

Salesperson Error

The team attributed some of the reasons for price variation to errors by Sales reps in their dealings with customers. This characterization made addressing this issue palatable for various functional groups in the Six Sigma team to make roundtable decisions.

As discussed before, Sales reps could commit low prices to customers outside their documented guidelines or prior to approval from pricing. Sometimes they requested extremely low prices for approval but offered much higher prices to customers.

IMPROVEMENT ACTIONS
The team recommended that any case of Sales error would require a trackable exception code to denote "salesperson error." This step remained out of control due to low detectability except for using detective controls as just discussed. The team proposed that an error would need to be signed-off by a sales manager to make the concession request eligible for processing.

Approval Delays

The price approval process was a source of irritation for both Pricing and Sales personnel. The Sales team wanted faster customer responsiveness and sometimes lost business due to approval delays. Pricing could not provide approvals within 24 hours in many instances.

There were many reasons:

- The analysis was time-consuming.
- The Sales reps felt that the approved price was not competitive and requested a lower price.
- Quotation requests from a sales territory went to the inbox of a specific pricing analyst in charge of that territory, so if the analyst went on vacation or sick leave, the requests could remain unapproved and pile up.
- The information required to process a single quote resided in three separate order-entry systems, two of which were not linked to each other. The pricing analysts wasted time to manually input data into the quotation system while increasing chances of manual error.
- In the pursuit of speed, the Sales reps often provided incomplete data required for processing a concession request. The general approach used to justify a deep discount was to state that the competition was offering yet deeper discounts. The culture of the company pushed for customer responsiveness and hence, it was not unusual for senior managers to weigh in to make exception approval. However, no one could track who had approved such exceptions and how many times.
- When Sales failed to submit quotation requests in the specified format, Pricing wasted time in follow-up to elicit critical information that was missing, especially competitive price to validate the justification for a lower price.
- Sales reps could escalate the quotation request straight for executive intervention without following due process.
- Pricing analysts had minimal, basic knowledge of product features and product application, let alone their perceived value to customers. They were required to contact product managers when there were large orders or custom product but occasionally took the shortcuts and priced by gut feel when product managers were unavailable.
- The requested price levels seemed to be always 3 to 5% higher than the competitive information that many Sales reps provided as justification for lower-than-guideline prices. This indicated it was fictitious data made up to follow a formality, which only increased the pricing analysts' burden of analysis.

A simple measure was to set up a back-up individual from within the Pricing team to process concession requests if the pricing analyst in charge of a sales territory was absent from work.

The issue of wasted hours of manual input that contributed significantly to approval delays was dealt with quickly by getting senior management support to a minor IT project to integrate databases of the order entry systems. This move alone improved efficiency of the pricing team by an equivalent of 1.5 people.

The team established timing requirements that approval requests pertaining any transaction less than $50,000 had to be processed within 24 hours, and those for a transaction greater than $50,000 had to processed within 48 hours. Exceptions to these policies were requests for which the price was above a threshold value as a percentage of list or for which there was an accompanying written (email) approval from a regional sales VP.

The project team tasked two members of the team to work with Sales and Pricing to develop, review, and refine the quotation request form, requiring only a few pieces of critical information Sales could readily provide. The rest of the information required for a quotation could be populated automatically from existing databases. This measure provided relief and was welcomed by Sales for allowing them more selling time and ensuring that the Pricing team would get complete information needed for approving requests.

The team proposed a streamlined approval escalation process that defined roles and responsibilities of various levels in the organization. Based on discount thresholds (discussed later in this chapter), the team developed a method for setting approval authorities for different levels of people involved in the process, that is, Pricing analyst, Pricing manager, leadership team, and so on. In addition, every transaction greater than a certain size or one containing custom product was to be reviewed with the product manager overseeing that product line. All stakeholders in the pricing process agreed to this.

To make sure that the process could be sustained and audited, the project team developed a system of exception codes to qualify what level of approval was received to process a quotation. There were exception codes that allowed tracking of scenarios, such as Sales Person Error, Customer's Walk-away Price, Approval by Price Analyst, Approval by Pricing Manager, or Approval by a VP of Sales or Marketing.

Gap Between Quoted and Invoiced Prices

It was clear to the project team that salespeople needed flexibility for negotiation to make speedy decisions. However, when the invoiced prices were found to be 30 to 40% higher than quoted prices in many instances (and in some cases even 5 to 10% lower), the project Steering Committee viewed this as something that needed resolution.

The quoted price levels were significantly lower (6% on average) than prices actually paid by customers. This showed a hole in the process that allowed Sales to sell at prices higher than authorized by Pricing.

There were a sizable number of transactions where the invoiced prices were lower than what was authorized by Pricing. This was caused by misuse of old discount codes that should have expired, but some Sales reps had found ways to keep them active in the quotation system.

IMPROVEMENT ACTIONS

Based on discussion with Steering Committee members, the project team decided not to propose any preemptive controls. Instead, they decided to use the quotation-invoice transaction data to develop exception reports that some of the members of the project Steering Committee and other leaders would review on a monthly basis as part of the discount dashboard review.

Pricing Guidelines and Analysis

Although Pricing had a documented procedure for processing concession requests, it was a one-size-fits-all approach that did not have much credibility in the field. The price guidelines were set at a national level without taking account of market behavior pertaining to sales territory, transaction size, or seasonality.

There was a large variation in invoiced price levels in all markets for every product family in all transaction sizes in every quarter. Moreover, there was high frequency of quotation requests including very small transactions where special discounts were generally not required.

These issues justified the need for building an analytical framework to instill pricing discipline in the organization. The team built this with the following:

- **Price escalation policy:** The team recommended setting up a three-tier price escalation process that would be communicated throughout the organization. The first tier was the responsibility of the pricing analyst. This tier was designed to have firm floors based on a set of criteria (product, transaction size, and region). A Sales rep requiring deeper discounts could call an analyst, who would refer to their tier guidelines to approve the request. Anything that the pricing analyst could not approve was automatically and seamlessly forwarded to the pricing manager, who was responsible for tier-two discount guidelines. The pricing manager had additional authority but also had firm floors to work within. She would validate that all criteria were met and why this was unique, require additional analysis, and could approve a lower price only within her authority. Any tier-two authorization on a quotation request was marked with special exception codes for manager approval. The request could be escalated to tier-three or business leader. There were no guidelines for this level, but any approvals were recorded with the exception code for leadership approval.
- **Set Price floors:** After viewing the information collected during the Measure phase, the team developed an analytical method for setting price floors for all tiers by region, transaction size, and product line. The team also articulated a process flow to review price floor guidelines every quarter based on changing business needs or adjusting prices for different seasons. The sequence of steps in this process are

Step 1. Review price distribution to determine price floor levels for each product by transaction size within a region.

Step 2. Estimate the impact on Sales if price floors were firmed at selected levels.

Step 3. Recommend price-floor rationale in business review meetings to obtain buy-in from Sales and leadership.

Step 4. Publish price level guidelines for all tiers in the approval escalation hierarchy.

Measurement and Tracking

There was a large amount of price related information and reporting but was of limited practical use. The reports were generated from dispersed databases that weren't integrated. In fact, there were over 200 active reports, but no one knew the owners for 80% of them. Yet IT personnel and systems were dedicated to developing these reports regularly and in many cases shipping them nationwide. On the other hand, the business unit wanted to track the "hit-rate" or ratio of quotations to orders within the month, but no corresponding reports or metric was.

IMPROVEMENT ACTIONS

The team brainstormed and decided on a two-pronged approach to address measurement and tracking processes. First, they surveyed the users of existing reports and gained agreement to discontinue a majority of the reports. Second, they chose a few reports that were compiled into a price realization dashboard. The dashboard included:

• Improvement in price realization shown as a monthly trend on a control chart
• Monthly exceptions developed on the basis of exception codes
• Hit-rate calculated based on the improved database capabilities (linking quotation and invoice data) during the Measure phase of the project

Communication from Pricing to Sales

The Pricing personnel lacked expertise in not only setting but also communicating guidelines to the Sales team. They interfaced with customers occasionally, and these conversations rarely went well. Salespeople were extremely sensitive when a concession request was rejected without a suggestion for a more appropriate price point. They also did not like members of the Pricing team communicating directly with customers.

IMPROVEMENT ACTIONS

The team recommended developing "playbooks" for training Pricing and Sales personnel about the improved concession process. The playbook covered key issues in a Q&A format explaining the process in depth and how analysis was used to set price floors by region, product line, and transaction size. It also clarified roles and responsibilities based on approval authorities and the approval escalation process. Finally, it explained how exceptions would be allowed but monitored with senior leadership. The entire Sales force and Pricing team were scheduled for training within the period of a month.

Risk Associated with Improvements (FMEA)

The project team studied potential failure modes for each step of the modified discount approval process. The FMEA showed need for heavy reliance on post-facto reporting, such as exception reports to reduce sales-person error or eliciting adequate justification for quotations and reducing the gap between quoted and invoiced price levels. See Table 12-1.

Table 12-1 Part of FMEA for Process Modifications

Process Step	Process Input	Failure Mode	Effect	Causes	Controls
Salesperson commits price to customer without approval	Price approval request	Behavior unchanged	Continued price erosion	Improved process not followed	Exceptions report; management visibility
Transaction coordination request does not meet time requirement	Price approval request	Behavior unchanged	Pricing analyst unable to approve request without due diligence	Improved process not followed	Exceptions report; management visibility
Price review at transaction level without complete information	Requested price level; new guidelines	Extra time required for review causes bottleneck	Approval may take extra time	Improved process not followed	Need to test process before implementation
Sales rep misuses discount code	Discount levels allowed for sales offices	Behavior unchanged	Continued price erosion	Improved process not followed	Exceptions report; management visibility
Pricing analyst/ manager miscodes approval condition by mistake	Review and approval	Human error	Misleading conclusions	Coding error	Exceptions report testing and review
Measurement and reporting	Quotation and shipment data for reporting	Database fails or employee leaves	Temporary loss of measurement and control	Employee attrition or job change; database failure	Have backup person so data control lies with more than one person
Management review and oversight	Review of exceptions report	Management reluctant to make changes	Process improvement fails	Management did not buy into process modifications	None

Monthly Review

As part of the Control phase, the project team devised a monthly review format for an audience that included many Steering Committee members and other senior managers. There were three parts to this monthly review:

- *Price review* to see how prices were improving because of implemented changes. The components of this were (1) a realized price control chart (without limits to look at trends), (2) price improvement towards project goal, and (3) gainers and losers in different markets, different transaction size categories, and different product groups.
- *Exceptions review* to understand the variety, the extent, and the reasons behind the use of exceptions to bypass the newly standardized process for price approval. Components of this were (1) the top 20 transactions with the largest difference between quoted price and invoiced price along with the exception codes, (2) overall revenue loss due to price shopping and misuse of SPA, and (3) summary of approval codes used for transactions.
- *Monthly action plan* with actions that senior management considered necessary after reviewing price trends and exceptions. This would typically entail two or three key actions for follow-up as well as a review of findings from actions identified in the previous meeting.

After the team finalized the Improve action plan, they revisited the "to be" process map with all the process enhancements including controls. The team presented the recommendations to the Steering Committee along with a list summary of actions and their expected time line for completion.

Final Presentation

The project manager created a presentation with 25 slides for the Steering Committee. The general manager of the business invited several senior executives not on the Steering Committee to attend the presentation as well. The presentation covered the results of the five

DMAIC phases with a focus on issues and their potential resolution. In particular, the discussion centered on the control plan. Overall the topics in the presentation were:

1. Project summary
2. Documentation of DMAIC phases
3. Recommend process improvements and next steps
4. Metrics for process improvements
5. Finalized control plans

The team now estimated that the project could generate incremental revenue of as much as $3 million through price improvement for non-contract business of the selected product line without any loss of market share. The sources of incremental benefits would be: (1) process control leading to improvements in discount levels and (2) process improvement leading to better realization of increases in list prices.

The project team ended their presentation by highlighting other opportunities in the future by way of prospective Six Sigma Pricing and other projects, including

- Developing system capability to benchmark discount approval to historical price by customer, customer size, transaction size, and region for each product line
- Developing documented guidelines for Sales personnel on how much up-selling (invoice price less approved price) was appropriate (the current project had focused mainly on price being too low, but price being too high had been left as a parking lot item)
- Monitoring sales performance against customer's commitment volume at their contracted price level and agreed upon terms and conditions
- Standardizing contract terms and conditions to allow system-enforcement and ability to monitor compliance

The Steering Committee and other executives were pleased with the recommendations and the early progress of the project team. (Recall that some minor improvements had already been put in place after informal consultation with the project sponsor). The general manager of the business gave the green light for implementation without any adverse comments.

Implementation

Following approval, the project leader, now in charge of implementation, started work on developing a process for setting price-level guidelines by region and by transaction size. The pricing team developed three levels of price floors, each assigned to an approval authority, namely, pricing analyst, pricing manager, and senior leader. After getting buy-in from the project team and Steering Committee, the pricing team was ready to put the discount guidelines and approval policy into practice. The pricing team planned to review discount guidelines with the general manager, VP of Sales, and the finance manager in case there was need for change based on the needs of the business.

The Pricing team started project implementation by distributing discount guidelines to the Sales teams and the Pricing analysts. Each sales manager received a copy of the playbook explaining the guidelines and the new discount process. The project manager and a sales manager together developed this playbook. The project manager held a couple of training sessions using the playbooks to cover each sales territory. Some of the members of the project Steering Committee came along to the training sessions to signal the importance of the project to the company.

The Pricing team had also developed a dashboard for the monthly reviews with the Steering Committee. The dashboard included

- National and regional views of improvement in average price level by month.
- Sales offices within regions that were seeing rapid price improvement and also those that were still lagging. Each month the report showed the top five "gainers" as well as the top five "opportunity" markets. If a sales office featured as a gainer or opportunity market more than twice in a row, the sales manager was invited to the Steering Committee meeting to discuss best practices or challenges in their territory.
- A comparative summary of exception codes usage in actual numbers as well as percentage of total exceptions for all sales regions. For example, the initial reviews showed relatively high incidences of "Sales Person Error," but this statistic started diminishing rapidly in the second month of the implementation.

The members on the Steering Committee, especially the project sponsor, helped create a buzz about the project. This helped the Pricing team get visibility from senior managers and preempted interfunctional resistance.

Epilogue

Three months into the implementation, the project manager made another presentation to the Steering Committee to document incremental revenue in relation to the project target.

The stated objective of $500,000 or 0.25% price realization was achieved in the first three months of the project. The third month after implementation coincided with the peak demand season, which made the Steering Committee comfortable that the process would be sustainable. Indeed, one of the executives wanted to incorporate the expected benefits of the project in a presentation to the CEO the following day.

At the end of the meeting, the project sponsor (on behalf of Steering Committee), congratulated the project team again and signed-off on the project leader's Green Belt certification. All members of the project team convened at a local bar to celebrate the completion of the project.

The best was yet to come. When Acme subsequently raised list prices across the board to offset increasing raw material costs, the company reaped the full value of the increase for this product line, but much less in others. In just six months, annual revenue increases reached $5.8 million for this product line alone, all of which went straight to the bottom line, exceeding not only the original goal of $500,000 but also the revised goal of $3 million over 12 months. The market share reports did not indicate decline in unit sales.

Acme has since implemented several Six Sigma Pricing projects and subsequently deployed pricing software to ensure standard discount processes across all product lines.

12.6 Summary

For Six Sigma Pricing projects, improvements typically take the form of controls when it comes to improving realized prices. For projects such as one on decreasing the turnaround time for price approval requests, improvements can be expected to stick if we use reports to track this time across requests. However, given the multiple functions involved, most pricing projects will involve a mix of pre-emptive controls (for example, published guidelines) and after-the-event controls (tracking reports, for instance) for improvement.

In the Improve phase, the project team creates a proposal to take the analysis to a solution that can help achieve the project target. The proposal has a prioritized list of recommendations, the result of the team's use, possibly with the Steering Committee, of tools such as the prioritization matrix or payoff matrix. In making recommendations, the members from different functions on the project team should develop a shared understanding of the risks, using, for instance, a tool like FMEA.

Designing controls as part of the Control phase is necessary (1) to check if the approved recommendations are actually being carried out and (2) to check if the results being sought in terms of process improvement are actually being achieved. Eventually, controls are part of the modified process to ensure that it is standardized, that is, the process takes place as expected and as agreed on—and therefore it produces far fewer defects than before due to lower variation.

The final presentation summarizes the objectives and issues along with their eventual resolution. It also includes metrics that reflect what the project accomplished. This presentation is really about the recommendations and related future steps along with preliminary or estimated benefits.

Part IV
Enterprisewide Deployment

13

DEPLOYING SIX SIGMA PRICING ENTERPRISEWIDE

He who has not first laid his foundations may be able with great ability to lay them afterwards, but they will be laid with trouble to the architect and danger to the building.

—Niccolo Machiavelli (1469–1527)

13.1 Introduction

How do we get stakeholders from different functions in a large company with multiple regions and divisions to align themselves to a common and consistent way of executing pricing strategy? One way would be to do a number of "small" (Green Belt) projects than a few large (Black Belt) projects partly because of the number of functions and stakeholders involved in each pricing process. There is a danger that changes to individual pricing processes via these small projects would be rolled back in the absence of firm leadership support. Still, the benefit of the broad organization (not just Pricing) having a shared understanding of pricing and pricing operations can be enormous. Therefore, it is worth doing enterprisewide deployment even if the only feasible way is to execute through several small projects.

Therefore, before deploying Six Sigma Pricing enterprisewide, we should try to ensure that senior stakeholders for pricing—executives for Sales, Marketing (including Product Management), Finance, IT, and even Manufacturing—are in agreement with an overall enterprisewide deployment strategy or plan for price improvement (via Six Sigma Pricing) and agree broadly on steps for executing such a strategy.

There are at least three reasons why starting with only a few "small" Six Sigma Pricing projects may be attractive to senior management. First, the impact of pricing improvement projects to the bottom line with even a small amount of effort can be quite high. If we assume that nothing succeeds like success, then this is indeed a good argument.

Second, a small-scale project will likely not generate much resistance initially, thus making implementation of project recommendations that much easier. After all, any Six Sigma project, whether focused on pricing processes or not, creates or tightens controls. In the case of pricing projects, tighter controls (seen as reducing flexibility) and increased transaction prices, which are both perceived as decreasing sales, generate resistance from those whose compensation is based entirely or mostly on (dollar) sales and/or growth in sales.

Third, small Six Sigma Pricing projects create a starting point for mapping processes and help uncover the sources and the nature of resistance within the company, which may not be apparent at the outset. Thus doing one project in one division in one geographic region could be argued as a stepping-stone for replicating the work in other divisions or other geographic regions. At Acme, the Six Sigma Pricing project in one division for one product line attracted much attention and a wave of projects in other divisions.

While these are good reasons, small projects lack the momentum of large projects and are risky when there is no clear pricing strategy or implementation plan supported by senior management. The main risk is that what has been done in terms of process improvement in pricing can be easily undone as well. Even if the changes are not rolled back, any replication in other regions or divisions may be stalled, defeating the purpose of doing small projects.

Different functions may put forth different arguments for undoing changes even after a highly successful pricing project. This is particularly the case if the modified process has not met the specific needs of these functions. For instance, the modified process, with its improved controls, may not result in an improvement in the organization's response to provide quotes to customers or to fulfill orders. Or, salespeople may complain that on an average, the modified process does not shorten the price approval time while creating more of a burden on their time when they could be selling. Others may argue that the new pricing process controls (that have already resulted in increased profits) in a division should be removed because salespeople have already incorporated these controls in their "DNA." Sales personnel finding they are "losing too much time" because of having to get prices approved all the time. (Recall that approval was necessary for the process before modification, but salespersons sometimes circumvented approval.)

These concerns may indeed be legitimate, and the modified process should not curb the entrepreneurial spirit of Sales personnel. However, rather than rolling back the changes, effort should be made to address their specific concerns through such measures as decreasing approval-response time and simplifying price approval forms with prefilled data. In the spirit of Six Sigma Pricing, the Pricing group must address these concerns through data-and-fact-based reasons, for instance, by comparing response times before and after implementation.

Pricing is an area where any two stakeholders will have three opinions on everything and with every pricing decision dealing with a distributor or large contract, whoever is louder gets to interpret or even re-create the pricing strategy. For instance, someone may argue for a 12-month "seasonal discount" for a major distributor or distributors in a bid to improve sales. Thanks to global warming, we may well have a single 12-month season eventually, but the working assumption right now is that we have four seasons a year.

Doing an occasional Six Sigma Pricing project, unconnected to earlier projects, may reflect the absence of a pricing strategy, not just the absence of a Six Sigma Pricing enterprisewide plan. In the absence of a clearly defined strategy and its implementation, all stakeholders will try to create their own strategy based on their individual perception of gains and losses to themselves, their groups, or the company as a whole.

13.2 Developing an Enterprisewide Plan for Six Sigma Pricing

If the company already has a pricing strategy, the following steps are helpful for developing a plan or at least a direction for enterprisewide deployment of Six Sigma Pricing for most of the company's products and services:[1]

1. Identify and agree on strategic pricing objectives.
2. Identify core pricing outcomes and related processes.
3. Identify outcome (process) owners.
4. Create and/or validate a pricing performance dashboard.
5. Agree on data collection procedures for pricing and related metrics.

6. Agree on Six Sigma Pricing project selection criteria.

7. Prioritize projects to pursue.

8. Outline a meta-process to manage the preceding steps and various pricing processes while tracking bottom-line impact.

Step #1: Identify and Agree on Pricing Objectives

The first step is to identify and agree on strategic pricing objectives. To do so, we need senior management whose incentives are tied to the company's profits, and for public companies, to the company's stock performance. However, even these executives need to be made aware of the importance of price in their company's performance and of the quality of revenues in terms of prices and gross margins.

Step #2: Identify Core Pricing Outcomes and Related Processes

The second step is to identify core pricing outcomes and related processes. Although it takes very little effort to make square boxes representing subprocesses and connect them with arrows, it is much harder to follow these in practice and even harder to ensure that others actually follow these processes. Indeed, there may not be a clear process at all, or various people may perceive the process to be different. Still, we can list "outcomes"—price guidelines for different channels, list prices for different categories of products, revisions to list prices based on market conditions, competitor actions, excess inventory, and contract pricing for instance.

Step #3: Identify Outcome Owners

If we can tie these outcomes to specific "owners" as the third step, we can ask owners to document the "as-is" process and variants. The hard part is identifying an "owner" who can make the final call given that everyone in the company not only has an opinion on pricing but also believes they own some aspect or another of pricing. The process owner will also find that different players want to tug at the process in different directions, asking for exceptions and modifications. Eventually through Six Sigma Pricing or other efforts, as each process is rationalized to improving its outcome, it will be the process owner's responsibility to ensure process compliance.

Step #4: Create/Validate Pricing Performance Scorecard

The fourth step is to create a pricing performance scorecard and/or validate the existing one, with input from Finance. Are we looking at only the average transaction price as a percentage of list price? Are we also looking at the "quality" of sales in gross margins? A simple dashboard can provide pricing metric(s) by division and region. As more tracking is introduced, process metrics may be tracked as well—which region is seeking the highest number of exceptions to price guidelines? The usefulness of the scorecard lies in chosen metrics providing clarity and detail to improve the outcome.

By contrast, consider our experience with a particular situation unrelated to pricing. The organization was meticulous about collecting data for many well-defined metrics. External vendors managed the data and produced periodic reports for policy makers. However, statistical analysis showed that none of the metrics had anything to do with the outcome of the process. This meant that the effort to collect and report on this data had no value. Still, the manager in question decided not to publicize the analysis because it would disturb the ecosystem of the personnel and vendors associated with this data collection!

Step #5: Agree on Data Collection Procedures

The fifth step is to agree on data collection procedures for pricing and related metrics. The data collection should result in a fair (unbiased) estimate of the metric, and error count should be low enough to be acceptable to all parties. Part of the effort should be to find out if the data actually exists and can be obtained with little effort periodically. Data collection should also be consistent over time so that at least the changes in value of the metric are meaningful even if the base value is less-than-perfect.

Agreeing upfront on data collection ensures that stakeholders will not argue whether improvement or decline in, say, the transaction price, is not valid. Without prior agreement, they may question the data collection effort either on grounds of measurement error or on grounds of changes in the data collection procedures from before.

In general, simpler procedures for collecting data that produce less precise values of the metric are better than complicated procedures that produce precise values simply because everyone can understand the simpler procedures and because eventually, it is the changes that matter. However, this is subject to measurement error not being so big that the changes are simply a result of random measurement error rather than improvement in the process.

Finally, care must be taken to collect attribute data such as transaction size, region, product group, and so on so that the metric can be reported by attribute; otherwise, useful indicators may get averaged out. For instance, if there are big discounts for large transactions (in dollar size) and small discounts for small ones, the average discount will appear quite good if we take an average (percentage) discount value across all transactions.

Step #6: Agree on Six Sigma Pricing Project Selection

In the sixth step, Six Sigma Pricing project selection criteria must be agreed on. These criteria may be different for the first year than for the second year. True, the first set of projects may simply be chosen for least resistance, but that cannot be the only criteria in the long run.

Step #7: Prioritize Projects

Next, with criteria having been selected, the senior managers need to prioritize projects to pursue so they can decide what to do in the first year or so and identify the next set of projects when the chosen projects are near complete.

One way to proceed could be to make realized prices visible across regions using a scorecard with chosen price-related metrics against the backdrop of sales and margins. Such a scorecard then gives incentives or provides checks on divisions and regions especially in any large global organization in regard to quality of sales via price. This may give them inducement to do Six Sigma Pricing projects themselves, adopt the same controls, or adapt these controls to their business processes.

Whatever projects are selected either centrally or at the region level, care must be taken to ensure that nonprice objectives like speedy approval of prices to Sales personnel are not ignored.

Step #8: Outline a Meta-process to Manage the Preceding Steps

Finally, as the eighth step, senior managers need to outline a process and identify owner(s) for reviewing and maintaining the seven steps just defined. Moreover, they need to ensure that the focus on bottom-line impact is not lost at the company level regardless of any individual project's objectives and its real or claimed benefits. After all, quality initiatives can sometimes submerge companies in bureaucracy.

There are many pricing-related processes so there also needs to be a process for documenting, reviewing, and revising these processes as different Six Sigma Pricing projects are completed. Senior managers have to provide answers to such questions as how process metrics are brought into the price dashboard or whether process changes should be rolled back or controls replaced by incentives.

Every company may have its view of processes, but it must have a way of tracking these processes. As a company grows through mergers and acquisitions, it will have different pricing processes in different parts of the company for the same price-related outcomes. The company needs a process to document and rationalize these processes rather than leave it to uncoordinated Six Sigma Pricing projects to standardize all processes in different ways.

13.3 Goals for Enterprisewide Deployment

Enterprisewide deployment is more than simply doing projects throughout the organization, and therefore, it should have a clear purpose. Not everyone is directly involved with pricing processes (although many functions are), so enterprisewide deployment of Six Sigma Pricing should not entail requiring almost everyone to do a Six Sigma Pricing project. The benefits and the goals should be clearly communicated for any enterprisewide change because such a program may be perceived as being disruptive. The adoption of a new process improves when the implementers know what is expected of them.

There are objectives that span across all Six Sigma Pricing projects. The Pricing group should find out from Sales and other functions if they are having problems or if their customers are noticing the improvements. For example, are the customers noticing an improvement in turnaround time of quotation of custom products? Regular conference calls or meetings provide opportunities to communicate success (or failure), not just through dashboard metrics but also through qualitative information by way of customer or Sales feedback.

When an organization deploys an enterprisewide Six Sigma program, whether or not pertaining to pricing, it should prepare itself for any barriers to change. More than manufacturing or other service area, pricing is a function where a few small projects would fare better than doing a companywide deployment in five continents simultaneously. This is important so the different players can get a lay of the land in terms of the objectives and the requirements of the different stakeholders.

For Six Sigma to succeed in a company on an enterprisewide basis, we need a committed and involved leadership, top talent, and a supporting infrastructure.[2] Moreover, for Six Sigma Pricing, we additionally need senior management's commitment to price with a view to maximize profits in the short and long run.

However, given the current situation regarding pricing even in much admired companies like GE, we cannot expect any of these before starting Six Sigma Pricing. On the other hand, success from a few small Six Sigma Pricing projects can help achieve these. Therefore, these four elements are goals rather than requirements for enterprisewide deployment.

Goal I—Commitment to Price

Getting an entire company to commit itself to price is a major undertaking and requires two things. First, all stakeholders in the company must understand their role in pricing processes and the quality of the final output of these processes, the realized price. Second, the company should ensure that existing incentives do not ignite conflict between different functions. Everyone in the company must see the benefit to the company and to themselves in supporting pricing processes.

Getting all people in the company to buy into these ideas may take time. It is best therefore not to treat this requirement as a pre-condition but as a goal while doing Six Sigma Pricing projects opportunistically.

Goal II—Committed and Involved Leadership

Crucial to the success of Six Sigma Pricing projects in a company is the willingness of its leaders to commit themselves to pricing initiatives and to stay involved with implementation. However, there is a chicken-and-egg problem because leaders may be more committed after they have seen the success and the bottom-line impact of a few Six Sigma Pricing projects. Small projects that nonetheless yield large bottom-line benefits are key to building commitment.

Goal III—Developing Talent

Having talented personnel in Pricing, Sales, Marketing, and so on would certainly help enterprisewide deployment and individual projects for Six Sigma Pricing. However, it is difficult to develop or identify talent in the company without having done successful Six Sigma Pricing in the company. The goal of the enterprisewide initiative should be to develop and identify talent in the company ranks. The talent may be pricing-related, or it could be specific to Six Sigma methodology or to managing pricing projects.

If high-performers in a business are exposed to Six Sigma Pricing earlier in their careers than later, they may better understand the benefits to be gained through the adoption of a Six Sigma philosophy, and consequently include them as part of their own strategic vision for the firm. As high-performers are associated with Six Sigma Pricing, it will become more attractive to talented individuals in Pricing, Marketing, Sales, or Finance.

Goal IV—Supporting Infrastructure

Infrastructure can take the form of organization, computer systems, and dedicated resources. Dedicated resources include Six Sigma specialists (Master Black Belts) that the company will already have if it has committed itself to Six Sigma methodology. The company may need a group within the program management office (PMO) to manage all pricing projects under the enterprisewide deployment.

These goals would comprise a tall order if we were to consider them as hard requirements. Moreover, installing pricing systems without developing pricing discipline as a result of Six Sigma Pricing deployment throughout the company might add to the chaos and variability rather than decrease it. But as goals, they are achievable through a well-managed succession of small Six Sigma Pricing projects.

13.4 A Starting Toolset for Six Sigma

As discussed in Chapter 7, "Tools for Six Sigma," there are many tools for Six Sigma projects. What would be a good starting list of tools especially for nonmanufacturing domains like pricing? This has implications for some minimal level of training to get people started with Six Sigma Pricing without incurring a huge starting burden.

To help answer this question, we analyzed a sample of 31 "Green Belt" Six Sigma services projects, both pricing and nonpricing related, mostly the latter, from among 100 projects that one of the authors supervised. Individuals, mostly from financial companies, undertook these projects with support from at most a handful of colleagues in their companies, based mostly in the financial district (the City) in London.

The majority of the information contained in the data gathered is qualitative, containing details on the industry of the firm in question; the objective of the project; Six Sigma tools used as part of the project; the targeted function of the project; and the recommendations resulting from the project. For a fair portion of the cases, a projected savings was quantified.

In evaluating the use of tools across the sample of projects, the obvious emerging trend is the relationship between the complexity of the tools and the frequency of their use (see Table 13-1). We found the most commonly used tools to be charts, including run-charts and bar charts—a likely consequence of the fact that these tools are simple to employ. The process map, a simple tool aimed at visually detailing the elements and hand-offs in a process, has been used across all projects. The use of the fishbone diagram is also quite prevalent, the next most common tool used, used in five of the eight industry sectors in our sample.

Table 13-1   Tools used in a sample of 31 Six Sigma services projects

Charts	Process Map	Fishbone	Histogram	Scatter Plot	Pareto	Regession	ANOVA Regression/ Correlation	Linear Graph	FMEA	Control Chart	Chi-Squared	Total
27	25	18	11	10	7	6	5	4	4	3	1	121

Our purpose in providing these statistics from services-related Six Sigma projects is to show that the beginning can be quite diverse, unlike manufacturing-related projects. Yet, the number of tools can be quite limited and not very statistically sophisticated. Thus, to start Six Sigma Pricing projects, a company can start with basic Six Sigma training over only 2–3 days along with an awareness of pricing processes.

13.5 Pitfalls and Challenges

Consider how individual projects fail, that is, their different failure modes. A project may fail because it has been abandoned soon after the

Define phase. It may fail because Define took so long that the project team went straight to Improve, short-circuiting the Measure and Analyze phases or doing the minimum to make it look like a Six Sigma or Six Sigma Pricing project on the surface. Even a properly completed project may fail because none of the improvements is implemented. Even if the implementation is done and successful results obtained, a project can be a failure from the company's viewpoint in the long run because the results are either rolled back or because the improvements are not implemented beyond the initial division or region.

Pitfalls and challenges for Six Sigma Pricing arise at the enterprisewide deployment level or at the specific project level.

Pitfalls during enterprisewide deployment can result in unconvinced or even hostile employees and their managers, blocking progress even for project selection. Pricing-related issues lay the groundwork for even more pitfalls than those faced by other Six Sigma projects owing to the number of functions and other stakeholders with different incentives that are involved in any pricing process.

Project-specific issues stem from the simple fact that any Six Sigma Pricing project is, after all, a project—a Six Sigma one. It is susceptible to the same issues that can make any project and, especially any Six Sigma project, fail.

Thus a company could fail at enterprisewide Six Sigma deployment at the very outset. If it succeeds initially, and many services-related projects get started, some of these projects could fail depending on how project managers and sponsors run their respective projects. Even if many services-related projects succeed, pricing-related projects can fail owing to the nature of pricing processes. Therefore, it is useful to be mindful of these pitfalls from the very start.

Pitfalls at the Enterprisewide Deployment Level

1. **Starting without an agreed-upon and communicated strategy**: Not having an operational strategy, namely a Six Sigma Pricing strategy outlining objectives, outcomes, processes, metrics, project selection and a meta-process is the

biggest pitfall because it means the senior leadership is not behind enterprisewide deployment and does not consider pricing to be critically important.

2. **Enterprisewide training without enterprisewide communication:** Enterprisewide Six Sigma Pricing deployment can fail if the manner of the initial training is done without clear communication, thereby generating hostility and even behind-the-scenes ridicule. Service situations, including those with pricing, are particularly vulnerable. This is because people in service situations may not be able to understand why some process improvement functions from manufacturing apply to them. Examples in Six Sigma training are usually taken from manufacturing, and these turn out to be less-than-motivating. The notion of a "process" and "defect" is usually much weaker in service situations, leading to problems understanding the purpose of Six Sigma in-services. This has happened with some companies seeking to deploy Six Sigma enterprisewide, forcing everyone to go through training without convincing them of the motivation and the results expected.

3. **Not recognizing the pressure to undo even successful projects:** What goes up may come down again—if the average realized price improves then there may be calls from Sales to remove price restrictions that eventually result in realized prices coming down. Zealous efforts—what goes up may come down eventually as previous gains are unraveled, owing in part to the incentive structure in companies. Eckes[1] notes that about a fifth of their clients failed to generate returns on their Six Sigma efforts. Our experience with Six Sigma Pricing indicates that the failure rate can be higher than that of Six Sigma efforts simply because many stakeholders try to roll back the pricing-process-related changes especially after successful projects. They may find the new controls onerous, or they may perceive that their individual or group incentive payoffs could suffer.

4. **Getting overambitious with starting projects:** A few large Black Belt projects or many small Green Belt projects? This is a difficult question. A large project, if successful, may generate a large impact to the bottom line but also communication among a diverse set of personnel from different functions, setting the foundation for sustained benefits. On the other hand, many

small projects mean some or many will likely not produce much result even though others may be quite successful, and people are likely to point out to failures rather than successes. However, large projects mean there are consultants in visible positions, and this may present a challenge in engaging people from within the company.

5. **Assuming success in companies otherwise committed to Six Sigma:** While many Six Sigma projects may have succeeded in a company, a specific Six Sigma Pricing project has its own pitfalls in the same environment.

6. **Leaving pricing to Pricing personnel:** Just as a failure mode for Six Sigma projects is to leave "quality" to the quality control people (thus leaving key stakeholders and implementers uninvolved), a problem for Six Sigma Pricing projects is to leave these projects to Pricing personnel. Doing so would leave the others to figure out ways to undo the projects' success.

Pitfalls at the Project Level

How projects and initiatives fail in general applies to Six Sigma Pricing projects as well. Some of the causes are

1. **Lack of senior management support for a particular project:** In particular, weak support by the project champion can be a major cause of project failure.

2. **Change in senior manager or champion:** This has the same consequence in that the new person may be less committed or simply be less aware of the importance of the Six Sigma Pricing project. Moreover, a new person wishing to make his or her mark quickly may have his or her own pet projects in mind.

3. **Key stakeholders not represented in project team:** For Six Sigma Projects in particular, stakeholders do not adhere to control plan especially in service projects.

4. **Scope of project:** Just as senior management can get overly ambitious with the selection of initial number and type of projects, a project team and the project champion may get overly ambitious, resulting in a project scope and promises that are difficult to fulfill. Indeed, given the nature of pricing projects,

there may be those who may encourage a large scope just to delay the completion or to let the project founder. At the other end, the project may be so small in scope because of the Steering Committee's restrictions on it, that not even the project team leader is excited about it.

5. **Scope creep**: Even if the project is scoped properly at the outset, it may be tempting to add more things later or to try to make after many improvements simultaneously to take care of "other" problems as well—even though these other problems were not part of the original scope. It is certainly tempting to follow up on all possible improvements, and there may even be good reasons, so it takes a lot of discipline to have a narrow scope and to keep it narrow for the duration of the project.

6. **Poor team dynamics**: Team dynamics can make any project fail, but pricing-related projects with team members from diverse functions reporting to different people are especially vulnerable. The following can prevent bad team dynamics from derailing any project: (1) run effective meetings with ground rules and a detailed agenda including desired outcome(s), personnel responsibilities, and expected amount of time, (2) agree on a primary and secondary decision-making method, that is, consensus and two-thirds majority respectively, (3) team leader and champion to deal with maladaptive behavior or other forms of resistance that would eventually lead to project failure, and (4) clear and regular communication within the team and with the project champion and Steering Committee—email is not enough![2]

7. **Pricing-specific challenges**: Continuous process improvement assumes a stable environment. Changes in the business environment challenge this premise because we need to keep adapting the process and appropriate controls. At the same time, the pricing process itself is under challenge all the time with new shortcuts or workarounds being devised.

8. **Using statistical tools without sufficient process knowledge**: Pricing projects tend to have a lot of data that may or may not be pertinent to the objective of the project. The availability of this data makes it tempting to throw the data at some statistical software to "see what comes out." The result is wasted resources, loss of interest, or even worse—loss of credibility

with the project team and the steering team. It is essential for the project leader to invest time and effort in the process and process-related tools.

9. **Design of controls**: The controls proposed by the project may be so weak as to render the entire project meaningless. This can result from either the project team proposing weak controls or the Steering Committee weakening the controls proposed by the project team. Even if the controls for the modified process are well-designed, there may be weak controls on the implementation of the proposed controls, resulting in inadequate or infrequent monitoring.

13.3 Summary

With pricing projects there is a danger that the improvements could be rolled back in the future in that these improvements do not by themselves change the incentives of the different functions. As such, rather than doing a few unconnected projects, it is better to have a plan for enterprisewide deployment with support from the senior managers of the different functions.

The following eight steps can help develop an enterprisewide plan:

1. Identify and agree on strategic pricing objectives.
2. Identify core pricing outcomes and related processes.
3. Identify outcome (process) owners.
4. Create and/or validate a pricing performance dashboard.
5. Agree on data collection procedures for pricing and related metrics.
6. Agree on Six Sigma Pricing project selection criteria.
7. Prioritize projects to pursue.
8. Outline a meta-process to manage the above steps while tracking the bottom-line impact.

For Six Sigma Pricing, we additionally need senior management's commitment to price with a view to maximize profits in the short and long run. As with any Six Sigma effort companywide, we also need a committed and involved leadership, top talent, and a supporting infrastructure.

However, we cannot expect to start having all these in place. In fact, these are goals rather than requirements for enterprisewide deployment.

Pitfalls and challenges for Six Sigma Pricing arise at the enterprisewide deployment level or at the specific project level. Pitfalls during enterprisewide deployment can block progress even at early stages like project selection. At the project level, a Six Sigma Pricing project is susceptible to the same issues that can make any project or any Six Sigma project in services fail.

14
THE TAKEAWAY

Treat people as if they were what they ought to be and you help them become what they are capable of being.

—Goethe

We summarize from the viewpoint that you want to bring about change and visibility of prices and pricing in your organization. We do so in the form of "messages" that you can take away with you.

Focus on Maximizing Long-Term Profits

This is a truism. However, many companies act as if their goal is only to maximize sales. The underlying but flawed logic is that profits magically appear when sales are high, but there is no evidence that margins will keep improving with more sales. We have heard different versions of this logic, so we believe that it is pervasive.

Another well-worn notion is that the price in a competitive market is dictated by the market, and that the company can do nothing other than decrease its costs to increase profits. It is difficult to imagine the "invisible hand of the market" efficiently correcting for price in over tens of thousands of transactions everyday in negotiations among parties, without perfect information about the others' needs or about the competition. It is no secret that companies experience a "hockey stick" effect of sales, profitable or not, at month-, quarter-, or year-end. Why is it that this invisible hand only occurs at quarter-end, even though both demand and supply are continuous throughout the quarter?

From a CEO's perspective, Wall Street analysts look not only at sales numbers in quarterly reports, but they also assess the sustainability of short-term and long-term profits. Showing price growth and sales growth would be ideal of course, and showing unprofitable sales in one quarter may be forgivable. But consistent growth in unprofitable sales is bound to hurt shareholders even in the short term.

Improving Prices Is Better than Cutting Costs

We have shown with examples that a small percentage increase in average prices has more impact than the same percentage increase in revenues or decrease in costs. However, to improve average prices, you will need better controls and, in general, improve pricing operations.

Data-and-fact-based Approaches Help Improve Pricing Operations

Data and facts take much of the emotion out of the discussion on how to or even whether to improve pricing processes. With different incentives for different functional groups, any changes may be seen as threatening. Data and facts can show the extent of the existing problem or the impact of the proposed process changes with greater credibility than hand waving.

Start Today by Listing Pricing Processes and Pricing Issues

List your pricing-related processes, though these may well be outside the pricing department. Then start listing issues via focus groups or brainstorming sessions. You can also estimate the losses to your revenues due to variability. If there are pricing guidelines, you should consolidate them and make them visible to all concerned.

You can also estimate the losses in revenues because of variability of discounts. For instance, look at the variation in your discounts by SKU/by order/by region in the last 3 months or 12 months of invoices. Now, consider the line items in invoices with discounts that are higher than the highest acceptable discount—how much more revenues would you get if the discount were limited by this number? Even if you believe that 10% of the orders with excessive discounts would have been lost, you would still get a significant increase in revenues. That may motivate you or others in your company to improve pricing operations.

Start Small and Consolidate Gains Before Moving Further

Starting with one project for one product line or with one type of multiproduct transaction is better than trying to implement division-wide or enterprisewide pricing "discipline." Starting this way can help all the players—Sales, Pricing, Marketing, Finance, IT, and senior management—understand possible outcomes and can help them learn to work with each other. The organization as a whole can understand its own appetite for, and interest in, actively increasing prices as opposed to sales. A company needs profitable sales, and higher and tighter prices go a long way in ensuring that sales are profitable.

Improving Prices and Pricing Operations is Not for the Faint of Heart

Pricing is a minefield, owing to different incentives that are not directly bottom-line driven. The different functions may understand their incentives and the relevant metrics but they also need to understand the incentives of the other functions. When incentives are diverse, controls are a better way of improving profits.

Even with controls, profits are not guaranteed as controls may be unsuccessful. And if controls are successful and profits are seen to increase, there will be arguments to roll back these controls because "they have done their job and are now unnecessary."

Gains in Realized Prices Are Easily Undone

There will be pressure to roll back process changes that have resulted in more price realization, and when these changes or additional controls are rolled back, prices can come back to where they were. The key to avoid this situation is to do small but connected Six Sigma Pricing projects to develop the conditions that will make enterprisewide deployment successful.

Need Clear Roles, Incentives, and Checks for Individuals and Groups

In any large organization, different people have different roles and different incentives. They may also need different checks on them to ensure they perform those roles.

Sales Is the Lifeblood, but Price Is the Oxygen

Besides the quantity of sales, whether dollars or units, you need to consider the "quality" of sales. This quality is measured by the price because that is what determines profitability. Having fewer sales with high profits is better than lots of sales that only produce losses. However, many companies worry mostly about quantity, not enough about quality. Companies need the lifeblood of sales to exist, but they also need the oxygen of price for health and vitality.

NOTES

Chapter 1

[1] Stewart, Tom. "Growth as a Process—An Interview with Jeffrey Immelt CEO GE," *HBR*, June 2006.

[2] "The McKinsey Global Survey of Business Executives," November 2004. See www.mckinsey.com.

[3] Bulkeley, William M. "Lexmark Slashes Profit Estimate, Blames Price War, Low Demand," *Wall Street Journal*, October 5, 2005.

[4] See Snee, R. D. and R. W. Hoerl, 2005, Six Sigma beyond the Factory Floor, Pearson Prentice Hall, Upper Saddle River, NJ.

[5] See, for instance, Bennis and O'Toole, "How business schools lost their way," *HBR*, May 2005, 83(5), pp. 96–104.

[6] Baker W., M. Marn, and C. Zawada, "Price Smarter on the Net," *HBR*, 79(2): pp. 122–127, 2001. See also Phillips, R., 2005, *Pricing and Revenue Optimization*. Stanford, CA: Stanford University Press, pp. 13–14.

[7] GE annual report, 1998.

Chapter 2

[1] Stein, A. D., R. A. Lancioni, and M. F. Smith. 2006. "Inter-Departmental Price-Setting In Industrial Markets: Organizational Perspectives and Recommendations." *The Journal of Professional Pricing*, 13(1).

[2] Stein, Lancioni, and Smith (2006).

[3] Diamantopolous, A., and B. Mathews. 1995. *Making Pricing Decisions: A Study of Managerial Practice*. London: Chapman and Hall, p. 53.

[4] Diamantopoulos, A., and B. Mathews (1995: p. 40–41).

Chapter 4

[1] Sodhi, N. 2004. How to Increase List Prices in Industrial Environments. *The Journal of Professional Pricing*, 13(3), pp. 24–29.

[2] Phillips, R. (2005, chapter 1).

[3] Marn, M. V., E. V. Roegner, and C. C. Zawada, "The Power of Pricing," *The Mckinsey Quarterly*, 2003, Number 1.

Chapter 5

[1] Wilke, J. R. 2004. "Price-Fixing Investigations Sweep Chemical Industry," *The Wall Street Journal*, June 22.

Chapter 6

[1] A part of this section has been adapted from Abhinav Gaur's bachelor's degree dissertation at Cass Business School under M. Sodhi's supervision.

[2] For a historical account of the launch of Six Sigma at Motorola, see for example, Larson, A. (2003) *Demystifying Six Sigma*, AMACOM, New York: pp. 7–18.

[3] Snee and Hoerl (2005).

[4] See GE's DMAIC Approach, http://www.ge.com/capital/vendor/dmaic.htm.

Chapter 7

[1] Pyzdek, T. *The Six Sigma Handbook*, New York: McGraw-Hill, 2003.

[2] Breyfogle, Forrest W. III. *Implementing Six Sigma: Smarter Solutions Using Statistical Methods*, 2nd ed. (Hardcover). New York: Wiley, 1999.

[3] Eckes, G. *Six Sigma for Everyone*. Hoboken, NJ: Wiley, 2003.

[4] Eckes, G. (2003, pp. 91–96).

[5] Stagliano, A. A. *Rath and Strong's Six Sigma Advanced Tools Pocket Guide.* New York: McGraw-Hill, 2004. See also, Hoerl, R., and R. Snee. *Statistical Thinking: Improving Business Performance.* Pacific Grove, CA: Duxbury-Thomson Learning, 2001.

[6] See, for example, Eckes, G. (2003, p. 56).

[7] If you do so, add a small random number to X to separate out the points.

[8] Eckes, G. (2003, p. 63) shows a one-page response plan as part of the hand-off document.

[9] We refer the reader to any book on quality control.

[10] Kaplan, R. S. and D. P. Norton, *The Balanced Scorecard: Translating Strategy into Action*, Boston: HBS Press, 1996.

Chapter 8

[1] Darlin, Damon. "Profit Falls to Half," *New York Times*, August 18, 2006.

[2] Darlin, Damon. "At Dell, Profit Rises, Questions Linger," *New York Times*, November 22, 2006.

[3] Darlin, Damon. "Founder", *New York Times*, February 1, 2007.

Chapter 9

[1] See for instance, Eckes, G. (2003, p. 30).

Chapter 11

[1] Eckes, G. (2003, pp. 42–64).

[2] Eckes, G. (2003, p. 54) calls these "open steps" and "close steps" respectively.

[3] Phillips, R. L. (2005, pp. 277–287).

Chapter 13

[1] Compare with the eight steps for a Six Sigma strategy in Eckes, G. *Six Sigma Execution*. New York: McGraw-Hill, 2005, p. 44.

[2] For Six Sigma to succeed in a company, Snee and Hoerl (2005) note that three elements must exist: (1) a committed and involved leadership, (2) top talent, and (3) a supporting infrastructure.

[3] Eckes, G. (2005), p. 120.

[4] See also Eckes, G. (2005), p. 107–109.

INDEX

Goodyear Tire and Rubber Company, 60
gross margins, net margins versus, 23

H

Harry, Mikel, 94
high-level process map, 107-108, 155
histograms, 112
  case study, 191-196
history of Six Sigma, 92-94

I–J–K

Immelt, Jeffrey, 4, 21
implementation phase
  case study, 216-217
  enterprise-wide deployment
    development steps, 224-228
    goals, 229-231
    need for, 223-224
    pitfalls of, 232-237
    toolset for, 231-232
Improve phase (DMAIC), 102, 202-203
  case study, 205-214
  tools for, 126-127
Improve phase (Six Sigma Pricing), 16
  case study, 50-51
incentives
  effect on price leaks, 32-35
  in pricing operations, 242
inefficiency of pricing operations. *See* price leaks

infrastructure support, as enterprise-wide goal, 231
input cost increase example (pricing operations), 79-84
inter-functional divergence of pricing processes, 11-12
interaction effects, in DOE (design of experiments), 114
internal environment changes, effect on pricing processes, 13-14
intuition management, effect on pricing processes, 14-15
inventory reduction pricing, 86-87
IT systems, complexity of prices, 31-32

L

leadership commitment
  as enterprise-wide goal, 230
  in selecting projects, 141
Lean Manufacturing, 93, 120-121
levels in DOE (design of experiments), 116
Lexmark International, 4
lifecycle. *See* product lifecycle
list prices, 59-60
  increasing, 74-75, 79-84
  modification processes. *See* modification processes
logit regression, 123, 189
loss of profits. *See* price leaks

M

main effects, in DOE (design of experiments), 114
management by intuition, effect on pricing processes, 14-15
manufacturer's suggested retail price (MSRP). *See* list prices
manufacturing industry example (price leaks), 28-29
manufacturing operations, pricing operations compared, xxi-xxii
margins, gross versus net, 23
Measure phase (DMAIC), 101, 168-169
   case study, 176-181
   data collection plan, 170-175
   process map, 169-170
   tools for, 113
      DOE (design of experiments), 114-116
      SIPOC, 114-115
Measure phase (Six Sigma Pricing), 15
   case study, 44-48
measurement processes. *See* review processes
measurement system analysis (MSA), 175
   case study, 178-181
measuring
   bottom-line impact, 228
   defects, 152-153
medical devices industry example (price leaks), 26-27
metrics. *See* performance metrics

modification processes, in pricing operations, 65, 72
   input cost increase example, 79-84
   list price increase example, 74-75
   new product launch example, 75-77
   product lifecycle example, 77-78
Motorola, 94
MSA (measurement system analysis), 175
   case study, 178-181
MSRP (manufacturer's suggested retail price). *See* list prices
multiple regression, 123

N

negative correlation, 125
net margins, gross margins versus, 23
net prices. *See* actual prices
new product launch example (pricing operations), 75-77
new product promotion pricing, 86
Nokia, 64
non-manufacturing situations, applying Six Sigma to, 99-100
numerical definition. *See* measuring

O

objectives. *See* goals
one-way ANOVA, 124

operational definitions, in
Measure phase (DMAIC),
174-175
operational level of pricing,
64-67. *See also* pricing
operations
ownership of pricing outcomes,
identifying, 225

P

Pareto charts, 113
payoff matrix, 127, 203
performance metrics
data collection procedures,
226-227
in selecting projects, 135-136
tracking, 226
pie charts, 110-111
playbooks, in case study, 212
positive correlation, 125
preemptive controls, 205
price commitment, as
enterprise-wide goal, 230
price controls. *See* controls
price leaks
examples of, 21-23
airline industry, 23-26
manufacturing industry,
28-29
medical devices industry,
26-27
reasons for, 20-21, 29
complexity of prices and IT
systems, 31-32
incentives and pricing
objectives, 32-35

multiple functions,
business lines, regions
controlling price, 29-31
price-value maps, 77
prices
complexity of, 31-32
levels of, 59
actual prices, 61-62
approved prices, 62
list prices, 59-60
list prices
increasing, 74-75, 79-84
modification processes. *See*
modification processes
product lifecycle, effect on,
77-78
pricing, levels within company,
63-65
execution level, 67-68
operational level, 65-67
strategic level, 65
pricing function. *See* pricing
operations
pricing objectives
effect on price leaks, 32-35
identifying, 225
relative importance of, 34
pricing operations, 64-67. *See
also* Six Sigma Pricing
clarity of roles in, 243
cost-cutting versus, 241
defects in pricing, causes of,
10-11
customer-responsive
pricing, 12
inter-functional divergence,
11-12

high-level process map,
107-108
stakeholder analysis,
108-109
for enterprise-wide
deployment, 231-232
for Improve phase (DMAIC),
126-127
for Measure phase
(DMAIC), 113
DOE (design of
experiments), 114-116
SIPOC, 114-115
Total Quality Management
(TQM), 93-94
Toyota, 93
Toyota Production System, 93
TQM (Total Quality
Management), 93-94
tracking processes. *See* review
processes

transactional level of pricing. *See*
execution level of pricing
treatments, in DOE (design of
experiments), 116
two-way ANOVA, 125

U–V

univariate statistics. *See*
descriptive statistics

value-stream analysis,
120-121, 186
variations, in pricing processes,
13-14
vendor-managed inventory
(VMI), 87

W–Z

Welch, Jack, 94

zero correlation, 125

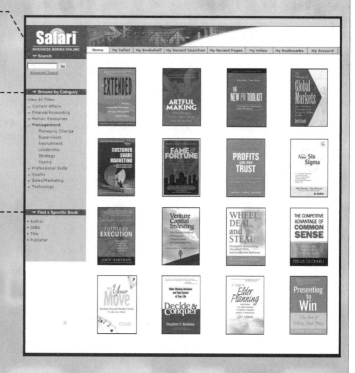

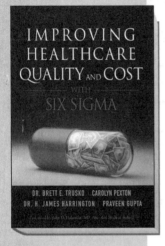

IMPROVING HEALTHCARE QUALITY AND COST WITH SIX SIGMA

Brett E. Trusko, Carolyn Pexton, Jim Harrington, and Praveen Gupta

Rising costs are making healthcare unaffordable for millions of individuals and employers. Meanwhile, 100,000 people die every year due to medical error. Healthcare must change—dramatically. Many leading healthcare institutions are discovering a powerful toolset for addressing both quality and cost: Six Sigma. But, until now, most discussions of Six Sigma have focused on fields far distant from healthcare. In this book four leading experts introduce Six Sigma from the standpoint of the healthcare professional, showing exactly how to implement it successfully in real-world environments. This hands-on, start-to finish guidebook covers every facet of Six Sigma in healthcare, demonstrating its use through examples and case studies. The authors show Six Sigma at work in every area of the hospital: clinical, radiology, surgery, ICU, cardiovascular, laboratories, emergency, trauma, administrative services, staffing, billing, cafeteria, even central supply. You'll learn why Six Sigma can produce better results than other quality initiatives, how it brings new rigor and discipline to healthcare delivery, and how it can be used to sustain ongoing improvements for the long term. Comprehensive and user-friendly, this book will be indispensable to everyone concerned with quality or cost: administrators, managers, physicians, and quality specialists alike. Where Six Sigma is already in use or being considered, it will serve as a shared blueprint for the entire team.

ISBN 9780131741713 ■ © 2007 ■ 496 pp. ■ $59.99 USA ■ $68.99 CAN

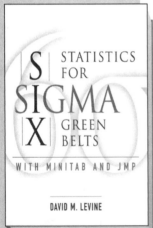

STATISTICS FOR SIX SIGMA GREEN BELTS WITH MINITAB AND JMP

David M. Levine

To make Six Sigma work, executive and managerial "greenbelts" and "champions" need to understand core statistical concepts and techniques—but they don't need to become professional statisticians. Now, there's a concise, non-mathematical guide to all the statistics they need—and none of the statistics they don't need. The author shows them exactly how to capture the right information, make sense of it, and use it to improve quality throughout the entire Six Sigma DMAIC process. Levine illuminates topics ranging from statistical process control and experimental design to regression analysis and hypothesis testing. Drawing on the experience that has made him one of the world's most honored statistics educators, Levine presents statistical topics with the least possible mathematics. Throughout, he teaches through realistic examples—including many examples from the service industries, among the fastest-growing areas of Six Sigma implementation.

ISBN 9780132291958 ■ © 2006 ■ 400 pp. ■ $39.99 USA ■ $45.99 CAN